Contemporary
Story

942

82)

i.

A WARSAW DIARY, 1939-1945

Michael Zylberberg

A WARSAW DIARY
1939–1945

VALLENTINE, MITCHELL - LONDON

First published by
Vallentine, Mitchell & Co. Ltd.,
18 Cursitor Street, London,
E.C.4

© 1969 *Vallentine, Mitchell & Co. Ltd.*

SBN: 85303022 7

Some of the illustrations in this book were reproduced by
kind permission of the Sikorski Museum and Polish Institute
and the Ealing Association of Former Members of the
Polish Underground; others were taken from *Menczeństo,
Walka, Zaglada Zydów w Polsce*, published by the Polish
Defence Ministry.

The photograph of the Warsaw Ghetto in ruins, by Robert
Capa, is by courtesy of the Iohn Hillelson Agency Ltd.

Designed by Felix Gluch

Printed in Great Britain by
Western Printing Services Ltd., Bristol

Had your law not been my delight,
I would have died in my affliction

PSALM 119: 92

CONTENTS

ILLUSTRATIONS

Introduction

THE FIFTY-FOUR CHAPTERS that comprise this book were begun in the winter of 1942 and completed in 1945. They describe the personal experiences of the author, but are inevitably concerned with the fate of all the Jews in Warsaw during the German occupation of 1939–1945. They are partly memoirs, and partly in the form of a diary; and are mainly episodes illustrating the fight for survival of the author and his wife.

I have not tried to present an overall picture of German oppression. This would be difficult, perhaps impossible. Some survivors of the catastrophe, soon after the end of the war, attempted to describe not only their own experiences, but the whole history of the destruction of Polish Jewry. This amazes me.

The idea of creating a permanent record of what was happening came to me at the end of 1942, when of a Jewish population of half a million some three hundred thousand had already been exterminated. Among those killed were my parents and three younger brothers, and my wife's parents and three younger sisters. I had the feeling that there would be no-one left to tell of the tragedy which ravaged the largest Jewish community in Europe.

In this diary I have tried to reveal the misery and hopelessness of one who did manage to survive, and the sense of the miraculous which, all that time, haunted me. Classical literature has often attempted to analyse the emotions of a condemned man, particularly in the last few hours before his execution. People like ourselves had a death sentence hanging over them for years. There was no question of reprieve. It was just a matter of time. But apart from dealing with the complex process of survival, I have tried to portray the characters I met. In particular, I have written a great deal about that noble man, Dr. Janusz Korczak, revealing him as a Jew and a humanitarian in an environment which rendered his heroism the more remarkable. It was a privilege to work closely with him.

In the last few years, I have collected evidence from about a hundred survivors, both men and women. Each tale has the stuff of classical tragedy within it, but many secrets remain.

While I was trying to escape death at the hands of the Nazis, I decided to record my experiences both in the ghetto and on the Aryan side. I continued writing till May 1943, when I suddenly had to stop. At that time I was working as a gardener for a Catholic family, friends of mine in Skolimow near Warsaw. I had to leave in great haste, but I managed to hide my notes and various documents in the house before I left. A break in my records followed, but I resumed writing at the end of 1944 and continued till the war ended. After the war I searched for the early papers in the Skolimow house; in vain. Twenty years later a curious coincidence occurred. An English tourist, recently returned from Warsaw, telephoned me with greetings from the family in Skolimow, and told me that the papers had come to light during extensive repairs to the house. They were delivered to me in London a few weeks later. When I saw them again, I remembered those writings of 1944 onwards which had been buried amongst a mass of papers. The two halves, now united, form the substance of this book.

The original Yiddish MS. was taken to New York, and was published in serial form by the daily paper *Forward*. I received letters from readers all over the world, asking me to publish the episodes in book form; I decided to publish in English first.

When I wrote this diary twenty-five years ago, I had one aim. It was to present a picture, however slight, of the struggle of an individual against overwhelming odds. Now that survival is a reality, it is important to remember with deep gratitude those generous Polish families who, despite their own problems, helped to save our lives. One family deserves special mention: the Piotr-kowiczes of Skolimow, who sent the original MS. back to London.

I think it appropriate here to express my thanks to my Editor, Nina Watkins, who is responsible for a large number of stylistic amendments to the MS.

Lastly, I am particularly indebted to my wife, Henrietta, who in spite of my opposition encouraged me to leave the ghetto. I felt that I should share the fate of the community. In my opinion, what happened to the group had to be experienced by the individual. Whether this attitude was justifiable can only be left to the reader to decide.

London, 1969   MICHAEL ZYLBERBERG

Warsaw Jewry: A Historical Review

THE JEWISH COMMUNITY in Warsaw is not the oldest in Poland. There are other towns whose communities date back to the twelfth and thirteenth centuries and who have left a wealth of documents to prove it. But the Warsaw community played an outstanding part in Jewish self-awareness which brought it to the forefront. In the hundred years up to 1939 it provided the leaders and spokesmen for all the Jewish communities in Europe and overseas.

Before the outbreak of the Second World War there were about 350,000 Jews in Warsaw, a third of the total population of the city. It was the largest single Jewish community in Europe, and the spiritual centre for world Jewry. The war made Warsaw one of the most famous and tragic cities in the world. The extermination of her Jewish population added to that fame, as did the hopeless, heroic stand taken by a handful of heroes in the Ghetto Uprising of April 1943. Warsaw will therefore be remembered by future generations as a symbol of suffering and resistance against tyranny.

Life was never easy for the Jews of Warsaw. The story of the community is a long sequence of combat and survival—the fight for existence and permission to reside in the city, for justice and some measure of freedom. This was finally achieved in the twenty years preceding the Second World War, only to be brutally ended by the "final solution" of the Germans.

The first evidence of Jewish official settlement in Warsaw dates from the middle of the fifteenth century. In 1430, Warsaw had 120 officially-registered Jews. The table which follows shows that after an interval of over 300 years, in 1764, Warsaw registered 1,365 Jews. In the years between, Jews tried, legally and illegally, to reside there. Records show that there were many riots against them during those years, incited by the urban population who, amongst other reasons, were afraid of competition and loss of work.

In 1483 the *Privilegium de non tolerandis Judaeis* was granted by the Duke of Mazowsze to the municipality of Warsaw, and King Sigmund I confirmed it in 1527. This prohibited Jews from living within the town. Hence the absence of data for the years between 1430 and 1764. Nevertheless, in spite of this decree, some Jews from other towns of Poland and from various European countries were spurred on to go and live and work in Warsaw, which held a curious attraction for them. Apart from its situation on the Vistula, which was a broad highway of traffic, they held it to be the safest and most secure place in which they could live as a tightly-knit group. Warsaw had always been a centre of trade, known to Jews for its contacts with other countries. They therefore sought ways and means of getting round Sigmund's decree.

There were a number of townships around Warsaw, the property of large landowners who were concerned with the cultivation of their acres and with the income of their tenants. These townships, known as "juridics", housed Jews who lived in the environs of the city. They were permitted to spend a part of each day in Warsaw, selling and bartering goods or otherwise pursuing their crafts. They could stay till sundown, as long as they did not take up permanent residence.

Jews were also allowed to come to Warsaw on market days, and when Parliament was in session after Warsaw became the capital in 1595. It was in the interests of many parliamentary delegates to have the Jews at sessions, since they had various financial transactions with them. It can be safely assumed that some Jews were resident in spite of the decree, particularly if it was economically useful.

Great changes took place in the pattern of Jewish community life after the middle of the eighteenth century and in the nineteenth century, when the fate of the Jews was closely linked with internal upheavals, political and national. Poland ceased to exist as a country in its own right at the end of the eighteenth century; it was divided into three provinces ruled by Austria, Prussia and Russia. But before the division, some influential and progressive

Polish leaders wanted to improve Jewish status and conditions and officially rescind the decree of non-residence in Warsaw. To this end many debates took place in Parliament, influenced by events in Western Europe and particularly in revolutionary France. But they came to nothing. After the tripartite division, the fate of the Jews was in the hands of whichever power occupied Warsaw. At first it was under Prussian rule, from 1795 till 1806, then under French influence from 1807 to 1813. It gradually reverted to Russian domination, which continued until 1914.

The enormous increase in the number of Jews in the second half of the eighteenth century was due to their loyalty to the Poles in their struggle against the various invaders. This made it easier for them to become residents of Warsaw. In 1794, there are records of Jews fighting against the Russians. There was a Jewish regiment which fought heroically in the suburb of Praga; of the 500 enlisted men, nearly all died in battle. At this time many Jews were granted official residence permits and their numbers grew rapidly.

Polish Jews showed the same sort of loyal participation in the revolts of 1831 and 1863 against the Russians, and many shared the same fate as the Polish patriots in Siberia. The years of the 1863 revolt are often termed the years of Polish–Jewish Brotherhood and Friendship. This era lasted till 1881, when there was a sudden pogrom in Warsaw. In the space of three days 1,500 Jewish homes were destroyed. In fact, at the end of the nineteenth century an organised antisemitic movement arose in Poland, which captured the popular imagination and created a boycott of all Jews. As a result of this the gulf widened between Jews and Poles and continued to do so until the Second World War. Thus a famous Polish writer, Boy Zielenski, wrote in the 1930's: "We live in close proximity to a nation whose spiritual aspirations are a closed book to us."

As a result of the pogrom of 1881, the first emigrants started to leave Warsaw. A thousand Jews went to America. Some influential Jews were against emigration, considering it a betrayal of Poland. The Polish press agreed with these sentiments. They felt the Jews should stay and assimilate. This attitude was later entirely reversed, and by the 1920's and 1930's many leading Poles felt that mass emigration of the Jews was the most satisfactory solution for all concerned.

The Warsaw Jewish community of the nineteenth century was not an obvious entity. There were the enlightened, rich and assimilated citizens, and the large mass of poor, hardworking, religious Jews. The city was becoming a stronghold of Chassidism and the Chassidic Rabbis had great influence on the masses. There was also a number of rich well-known Chassidic families who tried to get anti-Jewish decrees rescinded; this type of legislation was a danger to the practice of their religion and a menace to their very existence. Among others, the decrees that worried them were those forbidding Jews to wear their traditional garb and encouraging them to send their children to secular schools. The less traditional elements in the Jewish community felt that these decrees were all to the good and would help to bridge the gulf between Jews and Poles. This conflict persisted for years and was hotly debated in the first Jewish periodicals which appeared in Warsaw in the middle of the nineteenth century.

The late nineteenth century produced a blossoming of Jewish political and cultural awareness, as well as success in the fields of philanthropy and education, culture and commerce. New movements, such as modern Zionism and Jewish Socialism, were born. From 1897 there was a reassessment of the role of Jews in Poland as a recognised national minority. Varieties of religious affiliations developed, as did widespread cultural secularism; this lively intellectual activity on all fronts made the Jews of Warsaw the accepted leaders and pioneers in all spiritual matters. Really efficient community organisations, with Jewish leaders working together in democratic institutions, helped to create this image. So did the network of Jewish schools, both junior and senior; the many influential publishers of books and periodicals; the charitable undertakings which embraced all sections of the community; and the purely religious institutions which catered for spiritual needs. All this disappeared, and can never be replaced.

CHRONOLOGY OF EVENTS

SEPTEMBER 1, 1939 *Outbreak of Second World War in Europe.*

OCTOBER 1, 1939 *German Occupation of Warsaw.*

OCTOBER 28, 1939 *Compulsory Registration for Warsaw Jewry.*

NOVEMBER, 1939 *Judenrat Founded.*

DECEMBER, 1939 *White armband with blue Star of David made compulsory for Jews.*

OCTOBER 2, 1940 (Yom Kippur) *Creation of the Warsaw Ghetto.*

NOVEMBER 16, 1940 *Complete Isolation of the Ghetto.*

JULY 22, 1942 (Ninth of Ab) *Deportations to Treblinka Commence.*

SEPTEMBER 6, 1942 *Mass "Selection" of Jews for Extermination.*

JANUARY 18, 1943 *First Jewish Revolt.*

APRIL 19, 1943 (Eve of Passover) *Beginning of Warsaw Ghetto Uprising; final Liquidation of the Ghetto.*

AUGUST 1, 1944 *Beginning of Polish Uprising in Warsaw.*

OCTOBER 2, 1944   *Surrender of the Poles and Expulsion of the Population from the City.*

JANUARY 17, 1945   *Russian Offensive and Liberation of Warsaw.*

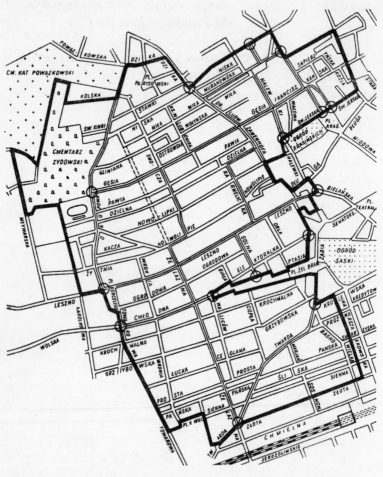

— The borders of the Jewish ghetto
— The "tramway"
O Official crossing points to the outside world

Plan of the Warsaw Ghetto

1. The Journey Home

AFTER THE FALL OF WARSAW, which had collapsed bloodily after heroic resistance, I felt an urgent need to go back and visit my home town, Plock. I wanted to see my relatives, but was also desperate to leave the capital city after twenty-five remorseless days of incessant and wanton destruction. We knew, of course, that Plock had fallen to the Germans in the very early days of the war, and had not been destroyed, but the people there had adapted themselves very uneasily to the new circumstances.

Travelling from Warsaw was extremely dangerous for anybody; but for Jews it was twice as risky, as the country was teeming with German soldiers. There were however, two routes, by rail or by river. The steamers up and down the Vistula had been active since the occupation, and I decided to risk the river trip, glad for the first time that I did not look Jewish. I could pose as a Pole, guessing (rightly) that no Jew would dare to undertake the river route since it was a long overnight journey.

Just when I had decided to leave Warsaw in October, 1939, an edict was issued ordering all Jews to register at the Community Centre at 26, Grzybowska Street. It was obvious that the list was being drawn up for the Gestapo's benefit, and equally obvious that everyone on it would be in grave danger. Only a few weeks after the list was completed, two hundred and fifty names were selected from it and the people concerned—all of professional status—arrested. They were to be held as "hostages", responsible for the return to the police of a Mr. Kott, a baptised Jew, who had escaped from Gestapo headquarters. Kott was to be found and returned to them within twenty-four hours. They could not find him and the whole group was shot. The Gestapo also searched the block of flats in Chlodna Street, where I lived, and arrested two of the tenants, David Milkes and Joseph Rozenberg. Luckily for me, I had just managed to register my departure with the concierge of the block and so did not appear on her list of tenants. Also, I had not replied to the edict, so I was not on that list either.

The steamer was crowded with Poles who were doing a roaring illicit trade in foodstuffs. Only "Aryan" Poles indulged in smuggling now, bringing supplies of food from the countryside into the starving city. It was an excellent business, but far too risky for Jews. I sat calmly among them and, of course, they were completely unaware that there was a Jew in their midst. Every time the steamer put in at a small town or village, a crowd of Germans burst aggressively on board. The word *Jude* was heard all the time, and they made a thorough search of all the cabins. They found no one, since no Jew dared come aboard at any of these remote places.

Before dawn we arrived at Vishogrod and the Poles prepared to disembark. They knew that the steamer would not move on till midday, and they wanted to eat their fill after the semi-starvation they had experienced in Warsaw. They constantly referred to a Jewish house where a "traditional" meal was being prepared and invited me to accompany them. I accepted gladly. On the way to this Jewish "restaurant" we saw groups of Jews being led to forced labour by German soldiers. They all carried spades and were singing—under orders.

The house seethed with activity. The master was bearded and wearing a skullcap; the mistress, in her wig, was busy setting the table. The meal seemed to be a royal repast—like a Sabbath dinner in a wealthy pre-war home. We were given white bread, soup, roast chicken, tzimis and fruit. It all had a dreamlike quality for me, though I ate as heartily as all the Poles; I could not take my eyes off this Chassidic-looking Jew and his wife and the laden table. After the meal, we all paid our host, who counted our change steadily and passed all the takings over to his wife.

After the meal there was time enough to have a walk before returning to the steamer, and the Poles took a stroll in the town. I remembered a former friend of my Yeshiva* days, who, I knew, lived here, and decided to go and visit him. I wanted some first-hand information about what had been happening in Jewish

* A Jewish institution for higher religious studies.

circles during the last few weeks. On the way, I saw stallholders putting out freshly baked cakes. This tragic and simple scene horrified me; it evoked such vivid recollections of the First World War. Then, in the small German-occupied towns, Jews had scratched a poor living selling cakes. Didn't the stallholders and the "restaurateur" know how immensely different this present situation was?

My old friend Sapirstein told me that conditions in the town were grave. Forced labour and the shooting of innocent people were the order of the day. Yet the mood was one of hope, however naïve and pathetic, that normality would be restored. People seemed not to sense the danger that engulfed them.

We went on to Plock by steamer. I was delighted to see my family, but immediately sensed the desperate position of the Jews. All their shops were closed and the stock confiscated; it was dangerous for them to be seen in public, so they confined themselves to their houses. In the streets everyone, both Jews and Poles, had to salute any German in uniform; the Germans had already started breaking into houses and looting and murder were rife. Saddest of all, perhaps, was the position of the Orthodox. They were ordered to shave the head and face completely, to remove every symbol of Jewishness. It was incredible to see these former Chassidim after transformation; many of them looked so utterly "non-Jewish" in the accepted sense.

I happened to witness the takeover of a Jewish bank by two very elegant German officers. They spent hours minutely examining the ledgers, noting all Jewish accounts, and then asked for the most important documents to be taken to their headquarters. The whole performance was conducted with the utmost courtesy. But the atmosphere was still that of a period of transition. Jews still persuaded themselves that this could not last.

Early in the occupation a fine of one million zlotys* had been levied against the Jewish community here, and twelve hostages, all prominent citizens, were being held in prison until the payment could be met. Among them was my uncle, who had been chairman of the community. The local Jews collected rings, watches,

* About £50,000.

candlesticks and money, but the current value did not amount to the required sum.

The warders in the local prison were Poles, and they allowed the hostages to receive visitors every day. Food could also be taken right into the cells. I therefore decided that I would take some supplies into prison for my uncle, and my brother, who had only one arm, accompanied me.

We carried a basket between us: I held one handle and my brother held the other, with his only hand. As we were climbing the stairs to the upper cells where the Jews were, a young, smartly-tailored German officer came down to meet us. I, with my free hand, took off my hat to greet him. My brother was unable to follow my example. The officer came to an abrupt halt, visibly enraged. He snapped, "Why didn't you salute me?" I answered quietly for my brother, "He has only one arm." The officer turned and slapped my brother's face. The sound echoed along the silent corridor. The German wished to provoke us into some sort of response and brandished his pistol—but we both remained silent and immobile. Our silence was neither fear nor cowardice. It required heroic restraint to remain calm at that moment. The German descended: we went upstairs.

The twelve hostages were lying on straw mattresses in one large cell, and were very glad to see us. They told us how badly they were treated, with frequent compulsory exercises for the elderly. We told them nothing of our recent experience.

I stayed in town for a week. Just before I left, posters appeared on street hoardings, stating that Plock was to become integrated with the German Reich. Its name was to be changed to Schrettersburg. It was hard to conceive that we were no longer in the old, historic town of Plock. We were now in Germany, in an atmosphere of growing menace. No Jew could leave the town without hindrance. He had to report to the police, whereupon he was beaten up and deprived of his property. After this indignity he signed a form stating that he was leaving the German town permanently.

I wondered how on earth I could get out alive. I was surrounded by people who had known me for years; would they point me out as a Jew? By a marvellous stroke of fortune, a German woman, who had lived in the German pre-war settlement near Plock, was also anxious to travel by steamer to Warsaw. Since we were old acquaintances, she agreed to accompany me on the return journey. When the German police came on board, they searched the ship and took off some Jewish women and children who were promptly marched to the police station. A soldier approached us and asked my companion who I was. She replied that I was a Pole who spoke no German.

I had seen my home town and left it for ever. I had said good-bye to my family; I would never see them again.

2. Janusz Korczak

WHEN THE JEWISH GHETTO was established in Warsaw in the autumn of 1940, the orphanage run by Dr. Janusz Korczak, the famous educationist, moved from its old location in Krochmalna Street to 33, Chlodna Street. The Chlodna Street house was in the ghetto, the former outside it. Number 33 was, before the war, a state secondary school with a number of private flats attached. Now, half the house was occupied by the orphanage, and the other half was retenanted by Jews who had exchanged their flats with the former Polish occupiers, since all Jews were now compelled to live within the ghetto walls. My wife and I were lucky to get a flat in the house. Lucky for two reasons. Because we could live in such close proximity to Dr. Janusz Korczak, whom I had known before the war; and because number 33 was one of the cleanest and best-run blocks of flats in the ghetto.

The new tenants were a very mixed community. There were very orthodox Jews, assimilated Jews, a few Zionists and Socialists, and even some baptised Jews. But our common fate and our uncertain future united us, and we lived as one family.

When we first went to live in the ghetto, Dr. Korczak was still in sprion. He was the only Jew in Warsaw who had refused, officially, to wear the compulsory Star of David. When he was released, he immediately assumed responsibility for the orphanage, remaining its director until the end.

He thought it important to brick up the main entrance to the orphanage. This struck all of us as rather odd, but he wanted to be cut off as much as possible from the Germans. Since his release from prison, he was very nervous, practically afraid of his own shadow; and our house was only a short distance from the ghetto boundary and the Germans beyond it.

The courtyard of the building became a central rendezvous, both for the members of the orphanage and the other tenants, especially in the summer of 1941. It was the venue for meetings, informal discussions and leisure activities in the long hot days. Dr. Korczak could sit for hours, two small children on his knee, talking and playing with them. The children of the tenants also shared his affection. He drew me, as a former teacher, into the world of the orphanage. My friendship with him grew even closer, as did my acquaintance with his deputy director, Stefania Wilczynska. He had few secrets from me, and was occasionally able to unburden himself about the difficulties of maintaining a children's home in such tragic times. Two problems were always paramount; to keep the children from starving, and to protect them from the outbreak of typhus which was raging in the ghetto.

During the year that we lived together, his children were well-fed and, miraculously, none of them fell victim to disease. Undoubtedly, the fact that Korczak was also a doctor of medicine helped a great deal. We were fortunate, too, in that none of the families living in the house fell ill. Not until the autumn of 1941, when the house was declared to be outside the ghetto boundary, did my wife become the first typhus victim. She was extremely sick for days; and on the tenth day, or thereabouts, the various doctors said she was beyond hope. I had avoided all contact with the orphanage for about twelve days for fear of spreading the disease, but when my own doctor refused to come, I became desperate and decided to ask Dr. Korczak to see my wife. He strongly disapproved of the attitude of my doctor, commenting that human life had become very cheap under our present degrading circumstances. He promised to help, spent an hour with her, and decided that he did not share the opinion of his colleagues. On the contrary, he held out hopes of recovery, and said that if Henrietta survived, we would have achieved a personal victory over Hitler! He regarded the struggle for life as a personal battle with the enemy. When I went into the orphanage the following morning to say that the patient was still alive, Dr. Korczak was as happy as a child and assured me that the worst was over.

There was one side of Korczak's character which was particularly mysterious, fascinating and enigmatic: the way he revealed himself as a Jew.

We established house committees in the ghetto to bear responsibility for the welfare of the tenants. Our committee in number 33 was composed of many interesting individuals. Isidor Krongold-Kronski, an active member of the Polish Socialist Party, was one. There were also Joseph Kilbert, a Talmudic scholar and former pupil of the famous Lublin Yeshiva; Mieczyslaw Ferster, a baptised Jew, the Warsaw representative of a Scandinavian engineering firm (S.K.F.); Dr. Korman, a paediatrician; Michael Schenker, an engineer; Herman, an industrialist, a relative of the historian Emanuel Ringelblum; and, most important of all, Korczak himself. I was the secretary, and therefore had close contact with all the other members. The meetings were invariably held in the basement of the orphanage, usually late at night, when the children were asleep.

Added to the usual responsibilities of this sort of house committee was the need to care for the orphans. This duty we shared with Janusz Korczak. The doctor attended all the meetings, leaning forward on his walking stick, apparently half asleep. One could have imagined that he was not at all interested in any of the items on the agenda. In fact, he was always alert and attentive to detail. He made his points stringently, without concession to the opinions of others.

On one occasion we were talking about giving a concert to raise funds for the orphanage. We debated endlessly about the programme, decided on the performers and discussed the language to be used—Polish, Hebrew or Yiddish. Some members of the committee wanted a Polish concert. Others opted for Yiddish or Hebrew. Dr. Korczak listened to our haranguing till far into the night, dropping off to sleep intermittently. Korman eventually passed me a note to the effect that Korczak's opinion should be asked. The assimilationists were absolutely certain that he, too, would vote for a Polish programme, since Polish was his mother tongue and the language in which all his books were written. But once asked, he slowly removed his spectacles, looked solemnly at us and said mildly that he was surprised that there should be any argument at all. He was amazed that intelligent people could waste so much time on so obvious a point. When one argued against the use of a particular language, one also argued against the people who used it. Could one deny, Dr. Korczak continued, that the majority of people in the ghetto spoke and thought in Yiddish and even died speaking Yiddish? That, then, must be the language of the concert—in any other the performance would have no soul.

His words had an electrifying effect. The discussion was ended and two weeks later the concert took place at number 33.

Korczak would often discuss the relationship between the Jewish community and the Poles. He felt that the Poles did not display any real concern for the fate of his orphans in the ghetto. He maintained contact with many Polish friends outside and they, in fact, often came to visit him; it would have been easy for him to leave and find refuge with them outside the ghetto, but this idea simply never occurred to him. He cared about the safety of the children, and nothing else.

In the 1930's Korczak had visited Palestine, and spent some time on a kibbutz. He returned to Warsaw full of enthusiasm about his experiences there, and gave some lectures about his tour. He obviously regarded life there as an ideal existence. Miss Wilczynska was, if anything, even more in favour of the kibbutz way of life than he was; she, too, had been there before the war, and she often spoke to me in Hebrew. She wished to get as much practice in that language as possible, as she hoped to settle in Palestine when the war ended.

Dr. Korczak found it impossible to learn Hebrew and had been unable to communicate with the children in Palestine. This was a

sad experience for him, as children meant more to him than anything else. He often tried, in the ghetto, to learn some Hebrew
phrases, but without success. Miss Wilczynska was mildly amused
at this weak spot in his intellectual make-up and regarded him
as a lost cause. Not, I must admit, without reason.

The conflicts which had always existed between Poles and Jews
were now magnified as a result of Nazi propaganda, and the two
groups were subjected to an inexorable process of alienation. This
affected Dr. Korczak's thinking and outlook. He became strongly
attracted to the spiritual significance of Judaism and to the Jewish
people as an entity, and he identified himself with every aspect
of the Jewish catastrophe.

3. The Golden Chain

WE HAD BEEN living at 33, Chlodna Street for some time. One
night at eleven o'clock, with a graveyard silence all around us
after the tumult of the day and four hours after the seven o'clock
curfew, we suddenly heard loud footsteps echoing on the outer
staircase. They were approaching closer and closer to our door.
Instinctively we put out the lights, sitting paralysed in the darkness.
Perhaps the dark would protect us, we thought irrationally. A ring
at the doorbell indicated that we really had visitors. Terrified, I
opened the door, and was amazed and relieved to see Korczak.
The elderly man stood on the threshold, apologising for the noise
of his old army boots. The lateness of his visit was due, he said, to
pressure of work in the orphanage.

I invited him in and he soon told me what he had come for: he
wanted me to help him organise a series of lectures for the children.
He produced a list of quite a number of well-known people who
had agreed to give talks: Dr. Schiper the historian, Stein the
philosopher, Rosa Simchowitch the educationist and Emanuel
Ringelblum, the future brilliant founder of the Warsaw ghetto
archives. There were some new names, too—people who had

recently distinguished themselves by their work in the ghetto. There was a representative of the Jewish police, the head of the ghetto Labour Exchange and some members of the Judenrat.*

I was, of course, most anxious to assist Dr. Korczak, although I felt uneasy about the last group of speakers. He sensed my doubts about them, and defended his choice by saying that he felt that the children ought to know what was happening in their new world. They ought to be aware, he thought, of their environment and the tasks of the people involved in this strange society. This aspect of the children's education had been fully discussed and debated with his teaching staff, and with the children themselves. It had always been his normal school policy—the idea of involvement and acceptance of responsibility.

Dr. Korczak said finally that I, as a teacher and a neighbour, should deliver the first lecture. What would be my topic, he asked? I thought for a few minutes and then asked for more time to decide. He wanted it settled then and there, so I said I would talk to them about the famous Jewish writer Isaac Loeb Peretz from Zamosc, who modernised Yiddish literature. He was very pleased, saying, "Peretz is just the right subject at the right time, and he belongs to Warsaw."

I got to the large assembly hall on time. It was buzzing with conversation, all the children present and waiting. Janusz Korczak and some of his staff were also there. He was sitting among the children, leaning forward on his stick as usual, his spectacles on his nose.

I began: "Not far from here, in Ceglana Street, lived the ever-youthful Peretz. He spent his life searching for ways to release the tired and poor from their labours. He suffered with the oppressed; he hated those who made them suffer. He saw Jews living in squalor and need. He lived through the Russian pogroms of the early twentieth century, and saw the desperate straits of the Jews in many far-flung small communities."

I illustrated my talk with quotations from his works and told the story of Boncie Schweig, Peretz's lovable character who toiled

* The Jewish council appointed by the occupying authorities to administer ghetto affairs.

hard, in great poverty, all his life. He was always cheerful and never complained; so that when he died he was greatly honoured in Heaven and asked to choose any reward he wanted. He asked for a roll and butter.

I continued, "In his later years Peretz discovered the joys of Chassidism. He saw in it the eternal struggle against poverty and lowliness; he saw proud men who stood up against their bitter fate, who tried to combat evil. And so he wrote the song of the great Jews, the 'Sabbatical and Festival Jews', who toiled for six days of the week and became kings in their own homes on the Sabbath."

I spoke in Polish but quoted from Peretz in Yiddish. When I recited the song "Brothers" in full, I spoke slowly, so that the children would grasp the full meaning.

White and brown and black and yellow, mingle the colours together; all human beings are brothers and sisters, from one father and one mother.

And one God created all; the whole world is their fatherland.

All human beings are brothers and sisters; this is what we must remember.

All human beings are brothers and sisters; black and yellow, white and brown. Their colour is different, but that is all; in everything else they are one.

All human beings are brothers and sisters: brown and yellow, black and white. Nations and races are inventions, a myth with no substance in reality.

It was easy to see that the audience understood. One of the children even knew the tune to which the poem had been set. I ended my talk with some famous lines from "The Golden Chain".*

> And so
> We go,
> Singing and dancing . . .
> We great, great Jews,
> Sabbatical and Festival Jews.
> Souls flaming!

* I. L. Peretz: "Plays". Kletzki, Wilna, 1922. Translated by Jacob Sonntag in the *Jewish Quarterly*, Vol. 1, No. 1.

For us clouds divide!
Heavens fling open their doors!
To the clouds of glory we rise,
Towards the Throne of Glory!
And we do not pray,
We do not beg.
We are great proud Jews,
Seed of Abraham,
Isaac and Jacob!
Longer we could not wait!
Song of songs we sing,
Singing, dancing we go!

Dr. Korczak looked round, scanning the children's faces. Had they understood the words?

It was long after curfew. The children were hurried to bed and I stayed on to talk to Janusz Korczak. From the ghetto boundary nearby we could hear the sinister, measured footsteps of the German guards. Dr. Korczak discussed my talk. He knew many of the works of Peretz, who had been a personal friend of his. The song "Brothers", he said, was so apposite that it should be taught to all the orphanage children and should become the theme song for all the young people in the ghetto. This, in fact, is what eventually happened, and in the following months we often heard it sung to a piano accompaniment.

The lectures continued for a year—all the time we were in Chlodna Street. Nearly all the speakers originally listed came and gave their talks. At the end of the year, when the orphanage was forced to leave the house for Sienna Street, and new problems accumulated, these activities came to an end.

4. The Burial

THE GENSIA JEWISH CEMETERY was as hectic as the busiest of the Warsaw Ghetto streets. There were hundreds of funerals there

Jewish policeman in the Warsaw ghetto, outside his district headquarters

Jews building the ghetto wall, October 1940

The author's identity card in his real name. This card was issued by the Judenrat, three weeks before the deportations, to staff who were "exempt from deportation"

Pages 3 and 4 of the above identity card, with the Judenrat stamp

Der Inhaber — Die Inhaberin — dieses Dienst-Ausweises	Okaziciel — Okazicielka — niniejszej legitymacji służbowej
Zuname Z I L B E R B E R G	Nazwisko Z I L B E R B E R G
Vorname M i c h a ł	Imię M i c h a ł
wohnhaft in Warschau	zamieszkały (a) w Warszawie
Eisgrubenstr. 17	Chłodna 17
ist in der Verwaltung des jüdischen Wohnbezirks in Warschau als Stellv. Leiter	jest zatrudniony (a) w Zarządzie Dzielnicy Żydowskiej w Warszawie
der Volksschule Nr. 17 Hühnerstr. beschäftigt.	jako p.o. kierownika szkoły Nr. 1 przy ul. Kurzej 10
Gültig bis 30 IX. 1942	Legitymacja niniejsza jest ważna do 30 IX. 1942
Warschau, den 30 VI. 1942 1942	Warszawa, d. 30 VI. 1942 1942 r.

Der Obmann des Jenrates in Warschau
Przewodniczący Rady dowskiej w Warszawie

I had quite a number of dealings with him and saw how hard it was for him to adapt himself to his new and painful circumstances. However, he held the job until the final liquidation of the Warsaw ghetto.

5. Masada Relived

DURING THE DESPERATE PERIOD of hunger, epidemics, edicts and notifications of new restrictive policies, when hundreds died every day, everyone decided that the most important thing to do was to maintain sufficient spiritual courage to survive and to help others to survive. Of course, this was not easily done under such terrifying conditions. The Germans watched and waited for any weakness on our part that would make it easier for them to create another bloodbath. Such was the tenor of our lives from the beginning of the occupation.

There were undoubtedly many thousands of young people who were anxious to offer the enemy active resistance. But this was generally considered to be impractical, since we were oppressed not only by regulations, but by an atmosphere of hatred, the direct result of Nazi propaganda against us. Each one of us felt restricted and unable to escape. Small wonder, therefore, that we concentrated mainly on spiritual resistance from the beginning of the war to 1942. No one could have imagined that the privations we suffered would lead to the mass murder of millions whose only crime was to have been born Jews. This passive resistance varied from one individual to another, according to his political, social and humanitarian beliefs. It was, in fact, easier for the deeply religious, whose faith was intensified, whose understanding deepened, and who saw this period of darkness as heralding the advent of better times. Such an ideal was not new in Jewish history, and an opportunity to put it into practice presented itself in 1941, when the Judenrat of Warsaw decided to organise a competition for a children's play in the schools of the ghetto.

We had three different types of school: those that taught Hebrew, those that used Yiddish and those whose medium was Polish. All three groups took part in the competition, except the deeply Orthodox Aguda schools. The Hebrew-speaking schools skilfully prepared a sketch of contemporary Jewish life in Palestine, with many songs and dances; the Yiddish schools, in their play, sought to stress social justice based on productivity. The Polish-speaking schools based their entry on extracts from classical Polish literature, exemplifying the ideal state when Jew and Pole would live happily, side by side, in a free world.

The headmasters of three of the Hebrew schools, Simon, Kirschenbaum and myself, could come to no conclusion about the type of play we would present, although we gave it a lot of thought. It seemed as if we would have to withdraw from the competition. Finally we decided to hold a meeting at the home of Rabbi Yitzhak Nissenbaum, a famous preacher and one of the founders of Zionism. We presented our problems, and asked for advice and help.

Rabbi Nissenbaum came to our aid at once. He suggested a famous Hebrew poem, "Masada", by Yitzhak Lamdan, which he felt sure could be presented in dramatic form. We were astonished. Masada was a mountain fortress where the Jews of ancient times resisted Rome. It symbolised defiance in the face of overwhelming odds, but after three years the revolt ended with mass suicide for the helpless defenders. How could we present such a play in our present circumstances? Rabbi Nissenbaum said quietly, "Take a chance. At least show that Jews have always put up a fight. This play will engender moral courage; it will demonstrate, at least, that people must stand firm." He took the poem down from his bookshelf, read fragments from it aloud and paused at the famous song about the chain which links generations and is never severed.

"The chain has not been broken; the chain continues, from parents to children, from father to son. This is how our parents danced, one hand placed on the next man's back, and in the other hand a Sepher Torah; bringing light to our darkness. So we, too, will keep on dancing, and our hearts will be joyful and lively. We will keep on dancing, dancing, and the chain will never break."

It all seemed so topical that after a brief discussion we decided to use it as our contribution to the competition. We were still worried, however, about the title "Masada" and Rabbi Nissenbaum suggested the alternative "*Gachliliyoth*", meaning glowworms. This would sound innocuous enough, and we knew that these creatures were to be found in the hills of Judea. This, then, was to be our title.

We set to, and our secretary Schulim Rosenbaum and his wife undertook to produce the play and supervise the music and choreography. The children responded with enthusiasm. Long before the final production, the main song about the chain of generations became very popular among them; they even sang it in the streets.

I had to translate sections of the poem into Polish for Janusz Korczak, who was amazed at the concept and the writing. I told a number of people about our play, including Yitzhak Giterman, who thanked us for the opportunity of seeing the remarkable production. He was a great personality who had been very active in cultural and sociological spheres before the war, and had a deep concern for children.

The competition was held at the end of the summer of 1941, and all the seats were booked. The plays were performed to a rapturous audience. The full significance of our play, "Glowworms", was not appreciated at first. But as it proceeded, many people became aware of the symbolic message, and were delighted with the use of coloured lighting to depict the glowworms of the Judean hills. For those who knew Hebrew, it was, of course, an added pleasure and a special experience. One could see that this was not just the Masada of ancient times; its spirit was being re-enacted in present-day Warsaw.

We won the second prize and had to give a repeat performance by popular demand. The chain song was sung repeatedly until the end.

6. An Orphanage Concert

IT WAS IN MARCH, 1941, that it happened. The house committee at 33, Chlodna Street had made great efforts to arrange the concert at the orphanage of Dr. Janusz Korczak and to have it performed before Pesach. Poverty and want were increasing every day, and we hoped to acquire some much-needed money. Dr. Korczak wanted to have a traditional Passover celebration, to which he had already invited a number of distinguished people, including Adam Czerniakow and his wife. The cost of such entertaining would obviously be high.

Two aims were paramount, then, for the concert committee—a high standard of performance and a substantial income. A number of professional actors and instrumentalists had been asked to perform and all of them were willing to give their services free of charge. But Dr. Korczak had also invited two other performers: one was a man often seen playing a violin in the streets of the ghetto. He was young, fair-haired and blue-eyed, and always attracted large crowds because of his polished performance. He did not have a big repertoire—Bloch's *Baal Shem Tov*, Acharon's "Hebrew Melodies" and some pieces by Grieg. He had come from Palestine to visit relatives before the war, and had been unable to leave. Korczak, like the others, was deeply moved by him.

The other person invited by Dr. Korczak was one of the many Jews expelled from their own small towns and forced to live in Warsaw. He became well-known as a singer of Jewish folk-songs, particularly those by Mordechai Gebirtig, the Yiddish poet and composer from Cracow who wrote the moving song *Es Brent*. He was shot by the Germans in 1942.

We, the committee, were anxious to sell tickets, hoping that this would bring in a fair amount for the orphanage. Dr. Korczak stubbornly opposed this idea. He insisted on free entry, saying it was better to trust to the consciences of the audience. They would donate lavishly, that was certain—and he was proved right. It was a great success, artistically and financially.

The venue was the assembly hall of the orphanage. Three hundred invited guests were present, the majority of them wealthy and important. Korczak sat among the guests and the children were ranged around the hall with the staff. It lasted two hours; there were items in Polish, Hebrew and Yiddish, the latter being the most popular. Oddly enough, the most assimilated members of the audience, whose mother tongue was Polish, were the most appreciative of the Yiddish songs and poems. Korczak's reaction was also interesting: he was overcome by the contributions of the two non-professionals and wept unashamedly. In later conversations, he often dwelt on this part of the concert, regarding it as a source of joy and comfort at a time of stress.

But the evening did not end there. During the tumultuous applause, we suddenly noticed Dr. Korczak up on the platform. We all thought he merely wanted to thank the guests and the artists, which he did, but he then asked us to bear with him while he read some brief poems he had very recently written. The concert seemed to be starting again. He drew a few sheets of paper from his pocket and started to read aloud. The poems were heavy with satire—they described a small black moustache, a large fat belly, a hunchback and, finally, an elegant dandy. Amid the scorn and mockery was a pervading regret that these people should hold the fate of many millions in their hands. He mentioned no names, but everyone knew he was referring to Hitler, Goering, Goebbels and our own hangman, Hans Frank, the boss of the "New Order" in Poland.

People listened and were horrified. Had Korczak gone mad? Some of them even slunk out of the hall and ran home in terror, but Korczak did not even notice. He went on calmly reading to the few who had stayed behind—the house tenants.

Afterwards, we asked Dr. Korczak how he could have done such a thing. Hadn't he noticed people leaving? Did he not realise that he was placing us all in terrible danger? He merely smiled and said, "The people who left are fools. What is there to be afraid of? Surely Jews can say what they think amongst themselves. Are you afraid of spies, or that someone will give me away? I don't think Jews would repeat any of this—they are all enemies of the 'New Order'." Undoubtedly, Korczak believed what he was saying. He could not imagine that there were Jews willing to tell the Germans anything that would incriminate their comrades. This was typical of his character: his standards and values were high and based on loyalty and trust. But during those first few months in the ghetto, he had been in some ways a different person: he could never have done what he did at the concert. His fear of people, of what might happen, caused him to brick up the main entrance to the orphanage, and he scolded the tenants whenever, after careful observation from the courtyard, he saw a pinpoint of light coming from one of the windows after curfew. When a German policeman came to the house, he was absolutely terrified. This happened only rarely, when the police found a wandering or lost child at night and brought him in. This pattern of behaviour was the direct result of his prison experience.

But in time he changed completely, speaking frankly about "the murderers and outcasts of society". The tenants' windows were forgotten and he was not afraid to denounce his enemies in public.

7. Three Sisters

IN THE THIRTIES, the three sisters were well known by their married names, Zylbercweig, Brams and Borenstein. They came from a religious family and their maiden name was Pinnay. They had been brought up in Otwoek near Warsaw, studied at various universities, and later taught at a number of Jewish secondary schools in Warsaw. All three were capable, energetic and known as outstanding teachers. In spite of their background, they later lived a far from religious life, being more interested in the absorbing political problems of the day. It is worth remembering that a facet of Jewish life in pre-war Poland was the gulf between liberal-thinking, educated children and religious, conservative parents.

I taught at the same school (the *Janina Świątecka*) as Mrs. Helena Zylbercweig until the outbreak of the war, and got to know her and her sisters very well. The three husbands were also teachers and the group lived as a very close unit. The sisters used to organise a summer camp for their pupils during the long vacation. This was usually situated in a particularly beautiful part of the country, either near the sea or in the mountains; I attended a few times, and this deepened my relationship with the group. Each sister had one child and these children, who were all about the same age, came with us.

In the summer of 1939 our setting was a beautiful village in the Beskidy mountains, not far from the Hungarian frontier. Not one of us there, neither pupil nor teacher, suspected that we were on the brink of war. We lived in a pleasant world of illusion.

The week before war was declared, we heard that there was going to be a general call-up, so we were anxious to return home from camp as quickly as possible. It was a short step into Hungary and we could have crossed the mountains, but we just did not think of it. In wartime, home seemed best. It required a great deal of skill and organising ability to get the camp safely dismantled and the occupants sent home, as there was already a general state of panic. We had to find two hundred seats on the train for the return journey, and thanks to the three sisters our efforts succeeded.

I cannot help remembering the sense of desolation among the few Jewish families in the village. They were poor, simple, hard-working people. Among them was an old man whose sole possessions were a wooden hut and a cow. He spent his day with his animal in the field, gathering hay and stacking it, and living just as his Ukrainian peasant neighbours did. His religious faith was deep and simple, though he could barely read and did not understand the prayers he recited. He had only one request to make to God, and he made it often in his hut and in his field. It was that a husband be found for his only ageing daughter. When asked what he could provide for her dowry, he would say with a smile, "I'll give all I've got; my hut, my cow and my haystack. That is all I have." He was sure that we, coming from the big city, would be certain to find a suitable groom for her.

When the local policeman notified each householder about registration for the army at the nearest town, the Jews of the village wept bitterly. They felt they were doomed. It was not the thought of war which terrorised them, but the knowledge that their neighbours were waiting for just such an opportunity to start a pogrom.

With heavy hearts, we, the campers, said goodbye to the village Jews and returned to Warsaw just one day before war broke out. Though the schools did not reopen, we, as teachers, kept in close contact. Hitler had chosen to initiate hostilities on 1st September, the first day of the academic year.

We often sat and talked—should we cross into Soviet-occupied territory or not? Everyone felt it was safer to stay put, even the three sisters. We were, of course, to regret this later. The sisters and their families kept their own comfortable flats in Zoliborz, a Warsaw suburb with very few Jews. They and another group arranged an underground system of schooling and prepared pupils for matriculation. The classes, held in private flats, continued for a whole year in spite of the risk involved. Our previous headmaster, a Pole, Professor Marian Odrzywolski, secretly collected progress reports and filed them, so that after the war the results could be publicly credited.

However, with the establishment of the ghetto in 1940, the three sisters had to leave their flats and the lessons came to an end. Their energy did not desert them; they set about reorganising another school for paying pupils. It was a primary school and they were lucky enough to find a suitable building, a convent in Nowolipki Street now vacated by the Poles. The sisters and their husbands started as the only six teachers in the school but gradually others were recruited, including me and Dr. Tola Krongold who taught English. Obviously, this was a hazardous job at that time; if anyone had told the Germans, there would have been reprisals of the most vicious kind, but the language was taught for eighteen months. Rich, fee-paying children attended the school, but each class had free places for poor children of good ability. We continued to function in the heart of the ghetto till the summer of 1942—the beginning of the end.

Two weeks before the mass deportations, an exhibition of children's paintings was held at the school. There were hundreds of visitors daily, including representatives of the Judenrat and other institutions. News of the success of the exhibition reached Gestapo ears. One day, a member of the Jewish Police came to announce that the Germans would be coming to make a film of the activities of the school and of the exhibition. When the date was announced, we were informed that both teachers and pupils were to come in their best clothes and bring with them special food and fruit. This film was never made as, at the same time, the extermination programme started, which brought both school and exhibition to an end.

The three sisters continued the struggle to live and look after their families. Problems of survival multiplied daily, and they confided to me on one occasion a reasoned decision which they had made. They did not want their elderly mother to survive merely to be transported to Treblinka; so they had resolved to end her life themselves. She, of course, knew nothing of this. They advised me to take the same course of action with my wife. She had been a typhus victim and she would be unlikely to survive if transported. They were willing to provide me with the cyanide, which I could administer without fuss. At such a time it is futile to give or take advice, so I listened and said that, for myself, I could not contemplate such a course of action. I found it ethically and morally repugnant. The thought of crime in the legal sense did not enter my head. A few days after this conversation the old mother was never seen again and no further reference was ever made to her.

In the spring of 1943 the Germans constantly advised the remaining Jews to vacate the Warsaw ghetto voluntarily. They were told to go to the two labour camps at Poniatow and Trawniki, both in the Lublin district, where they and their families could spend the rest of the war in peace and quiet. I discussed this idea with the three sisters. Because conditions were so hopeless, they felt we should all go there together. However, in the light of previous experience with the Germans, I felt that such a move would be suicidal. I was also influenced by the fact that my wife was now over on the Aryan side and I hoped to get across. Two of the sisters and their husbands and children went to Poniatow while the third family managed to escape to the Aryan side.

In Poniatow, the end came in the autumn of 1943. All the Jews were shot, falling into prepared mass graves. The third family survived longer, having been hidden by Poles; by accident, a milkman discovered them and informed the Germans. They were immediately shot.

8. The Last Yom Kippur

THE SUMMER OF 1941 was a tragic one, with typhus and hunger rife in the ghetto. Survival was a time-consuming occupation, and day after monotonous day passed. Oddly enough, one cannot help remembering the beginning of the German offensive in Russia. When we first heard about the impending campaign we were filled with hope, visualising a massive German defeat. Unfortunately, even in the early days the news from the front proclaimed a series of German victories with large areas of captured territory. There was sorrow in every home in the ghetto as we listened to the loudspeakers in the streets. We also heard vague, disquieting news about the slaughter of Jewish communities in the East.

At the same time there was an abundance of tragi-comedy, played out against this backcloth of devastation. A half-demented man could always be seen scampering down the street, gesticulating and yelling, "Roosevelt has just phoned Winston Churchill to say, 'Hang on, old chap.' "

There was a poor widow in the ghetto with numerous offspring. Her room was cold, and food was non-existent, so one of the sons, ten years old, decided to become breadwinner. He would run along the streets with a box strapped to his chest, shouting his wares. These consisted of stars of David, saccharine tablets and morsels of bread, all dire necessities. Suddenly an SS man appeared, attacked the boy viciously, scattered the contents of his box and left him crying in the mud. His mother, half hidden in a nearby doorway, had witnessed the incident. As soon as the SS man had gone she went up to the boy, saying briskly, "Don't cry. Stand up, put on your hat and behave like a Jew. Tomorrow is another day, you know."

The High Holydays were approaching and the streets were filled with scurrying people. All the synagogues were shut and the cantors were singing their prayers in the street. Dr. Korczak would stop and listen to the singing and the actual words of the prayers; I had to translate them into Polish for him. He was particularly moved by the cantor who slowly pushed a pram in which his paralysed wife was lying; there was no one to leave her with at home. He sang loudly, "The soul is Thine, and the body is Thy work; have pity on Thy labour."

A family group, a very religious man and his children, also affected him deeply. They could not sing and, to earn some money, simply recited a psalm. They had a regular pitch at the corner of the street and a collecting-tin held out in front of them, and used to render Psalm 69 with such feeling that everyone could understand their personal sorrow:

> Save me, O God; for the waters are come in unto my soul.
> I sink in deep mire, where there is no standing:
> I am come into deep waters, where the floods overflow me.
> They that hate me without a cause are more than the hairs of
>   mine head: they that would destroy me, being mine enemies
>   wrongfully, are mighty.
> Let not them that wait on thee, O Lord God of hosts, be
>   ashamed for my sake: let not those that seek thee be confounded
>   for my sake, O God of Israel.
> They that sit in the gate speak against me; and I was the song of
>   the drunkards.
> O God, in the multitude of thy mercy hear me, in the truth of
>   thy salvation.
> Deliver me out of the mire, and let me not sink: let me be
>   delivered from them that hate me, and out of the deep waters.
> And hide not thy face from thy servant; for I am in trouble, hear
>   me speedily.

Pour out thine indignation upon them, and let thy wrathful anger
take hold of them.

Let them be blotted out of the book of the living, and not be
written with the righteous.

For God will save Zion, and will build the cities of Judah: that
they may dwell there, and have it in possession.

A few weeks before Rosh Hashana (the Jewish New Year)
Janusz Korczak visited us at home with a new idea. He wanted me
to help him organise services at the orphanage. It would be easy,
he thought, to get one of the street-singing cantors, and he was
willing to pay well. I was astonished. Everyone knew Korczak
was far from religious. He saw my surprised expression and, not
waiting for questions, said, "At this particular time it is important
to hold services at the orphanage. The prayers may give people a
spiritual uplift in these tragic times. Of course, no one will be
forced to attend." He meant of course the children, who were
given individual freedom of choice in matters of religious ob-
servance.

Korczak added that the sale of tickets for seats at the services
might also bring in a large amount for the orphanage, but he
had another object in mind. He was afraid of introducing typhus
into the orphanage and felt that the sale of tickets would deter
poorer people from coming. I said I would help, and asked to be
kept informed how the seats were going. I got a letter a few days
later from Dr. Korczak. It ran:

Dear Mr. Zylberberg,

For many reasons we would like services to be held here on the
High Holydays. Various people have suggested that what should be
solemn and holy might turn out quite differently. If Mr. X. cannot
raise a small sum for the orphanage, how can we trust him to organise the more important details? The attitude of the staff is clear—
the director himself must decide. This imposes a great responsibility
on me; I must do the job meticulously. The final decision is mine.

Yours sincerely,

Korczak, Director.

It was dated 29th August, 1941. I still do not know who Mr. X.
was.

Within a few days everything was arranged. I found a good cantor who had been deported from one of the small towns, and got a great deal of satisfaction out of helping the children in this way. The children themselves got the hall ready. They laid down carpets and decorated the place with flowers smuggled from outside the ghetto. An ark and embroidered cover were obtained, and two scrolls. Seats were arranged in rows. The hall really looked like a synagogue and it was difficult to believe that the transformation had been possible in such an environment. The dignified atmosphere was enhanced by the silver candlesticks, the flowers and the general solemnity. Apart from the children and some of the staff, two official members of the Judenrat, the house tenants, and two well-known businessmen bought tickets. Korczak was pleased at the failure of the ticket-selling venture. He would spend all his time in the hall amongst the children, standing in a corner well back from the front rows with a Polish prayer book in his hand, incongruously garbed in an old grey overcoat, army boots and a silk skullcap. He was deep in prayer.

The cantor, who had suffered a great deal and was a man of learning, put all his heart into his performance. His supplications sprang from personal experience, and never had an audience been so carried away as this one. No one stirred. Even the children were glued to their seats. He recited:

> On the First Day of the Year it is inscribed,
> And on the Day of Atonement the decree is sealed,
> How many shall pass away and how many shall be born,
> Who shall live and who shall die . . .

Even the youngest were electrified.

Dr. Korczak had asked me to deliver the sermons to the children and I had refused, so he did so: one for the New Year and one on Yom Kippur (the Day of Atonement). Some of the words are etched on my memory. "As for man, he is from the dust and to the dust will he return". It was with these words, in Polish, that he opened on Yom Kippur. "This does not mean that we should give up hope for a better tomorrow. We are far from pessimistic. Life has a deep meaning, and he who suffers most clings most tenaciously to life. This applies to nations as well as individuals; Jews have always suffered more than other nations, and so their will to live is stronger. What are we praying for today? We are praying for one year of life. We will surely live and survive to enjoy a new life which will bury the old."

After the last evening service I was in a hurry to get home, but Korczak detained me. He said his sermon had been mainly for the children. He did not want them to be troubled. "But," he said, "I am afraid of what could happen. They, the Germans, are capable of anything."

This was the last Yom Kippur celebrated by Dr. Korczak and his children. On a sunny day in August, 1942, the orphanage was surrounded by SS officers; Korczak, his staff and his children (about 120 of them) were taken to the *Umschlagplatz*★ for transportation to the Treblinka extermination camp. Korczak knew, without a doubt, what awaited them; but although the Germans offered him his personal freedom, he chose to go to the death camp with the children. His one aim was to hide the truth from them and comfort them. They marched very slowly, in rows of four; I stood at a nearby window and watched them go. I never saw them again.

9. Death of a Convert

IT WAS THE WINTER OF 1941–1942. Typhus was spreading like a forest fire and thousands were dying every day. One could be fit and active one day and dead the next. This happened to a friend of ours, Mieczyslaw Ferster, a convert to Catholicism who had been forced to enter the ghetto with his family. I had got to know him when we were neighbours at 33, Chlodna Street; he had been a director of the Swedish firm S.K.F., in Warsaw, before the war.

During the year when we were neighbours he went out of his

★ Round-up and departure station at the ghetto, with a railway line leading direct to Treblinka.

way to demonstrate how Jewish he felt. He told me that his family had been observant Jews, particularly his father. He wanted to drive this point home, though I avoided discussing religion with him, feeling it to be tactless in the extreme. Ferster was a gentle, modest man, who got on well with all his neighbours, particularly those who lived orthodox Jewish lives along the "old lines". In addition, he made a special friend of Joseph Kilbert, a former student of the famous Lublin Yeshiva who was caretaker in our house. It was strange to see these two together, the scholar from Lublin and the convert. They often sat in the damp cellar which served as the Kilberts' family flat. The Kilberts, refugees from the country, thought themselves lucky to be employed as caretakers.

From time to time Mieczyslaw Ferster talked to me about Joseph Kilbert. He praised his intelligence, quick wits and nobility of character. This gave him the cue to talk happily about his own religious family. It was perhaps the first time that he had been in close contact with a religious man of such striking personality.

While the services at Dr. Korczak's orphanage were being arranged, I did not tell Ferster about them—nor, indeed, any of the other converts. I thought it would be more diplomatic not to do so. It so happened that Ferster was very upset at not being informed, and particularly regretted missing the Kol-Nidre* service. He often complained to me and said that he could not forgive me for my silence.

After 33, Chlodna Street was excluded from the ghetto, the tenants were dispersed. Conditions for all of us were now harder than they had ever been. Shortly afterwards, I heard that Mieczy-slaw Ferster was ill with typhus and that he wished to see me. I was not particularly worried about catching the disease, so I went along. During our chat, he assured me that his fever was not a symptom of illness and that his condition was not too serious. His doctor had assured him of this. Nevertheless, he wanted me to know that he still felt very Jewish and always would until he died. This was why he had sent for me. I made light of his condition and said goodbye, expressing the wish that we would meet soon.

* The opening words of the Evening Service commencing the Day of Atonement. (The Jewish day runs from sunset to sunset.)

Three days later, on Saturday morning, one of Korczak's children brought me the news of Ferster's death and added that Dr. Korczak wished to see me. I went immediately to 16, Sienna Street, the new premises of the orphanage. The change of atmosphere was obvious; the place was dirty and untidy, and Korczak was transformed too. He was harassed, sad and lost. He wanted me to go and talk to Ferster's widow, and persuade her to let him be buried in the Jewish cemetery. Many of his personal friends felt the same way, Korczak said, and they were sure that I could influence the widow. I promised to do my best.

That evening, rather unhappily, I went to see Mrs. Ferster. In the flat I met the Catholic undertakers, two men from the Aryan side* who had come to lay out the corpse. The atmosphere oppressed me; I could hardly approach the widow in the circumstances. It was obvious that I would be making a fool of myself. She made one request: that I, as a close friend of her late husband, should wait with her until the body had been removed to the church. I did so, though I felt very uncomfortable. Meanwhile, the two undertakers proceeded with their work, and I watched the scene for the first time in my life. They shaved the corpse's face and dressed him in a white shirt, black bow tie, black dinner jacket and black patent shoes before they laid him in his coffin. As soon as they had taken him away I slunk out of the house, feeling depressed and frustrated. The funeral was to be at midday on Tuesday, at the ghetto's Catholic church in Leszno Street.

Janusz Korczak, Miss Wilczynska, my lodger Gisella Hernes-Neufeld and other friends of the dead man were very upset. It seemed incongruous to them that arrangements had been made for a Catholic funeral and that Ferster would lie in a Catholic cemetery. They had wanted his last resting-place to be among his fellow Jews—an affirmation of common suffering.

The former neighbours at number 33 decided to come to this unusual funeral. The hearse in front of the church was drawn by two large, sleek, black horses. The noise in the street, augmented by children's wails and beggars' cries, was indescribable. Even the

* The whole of Warsaw excluding the Jewish ghetto, i.e. the part where the civilian Polish population and the Germans resided.

horses seemed anxious to get away. Fancifully, they seemed unable to look at the starving children around them.

In the church, the priest, who was also of Jewish descent, was conducting the requiem. The mournful chant of the funeral service and the sound of the last rites seemed to embrace the Jewish tragedy outside the church as well as the dead man inside it. The priest's monotone was constantly punctuated by the noises in the street; the cries of the hungry and dying mingled with the requiem for the dead.

The former neighbours from number 33, who were standing round the coffin paying their last respects, acted as pall-bearers. One friend was missing—Joseph Kilbert. He would not go into the church but waited in the porch until the coffin was brought out. This, he felt, was an adequate tribute. We, meanwhile, carried out the corpse and put it into the hearse. The horses immediately sprang to life, anxious to leave the bleakness and desolation behind them.

The tragedy of the converts in the ghetto was perhaps even greater than ours. They suffered as Jews and finally died as Jews, unable to resolve the terrible dichotomy created by their religious and philosophical conflicts. Their suffering took on a different quality. For us it was an inevitable adjunct of our heritage; for them it was an additional burden, an unrelieved trauma. The only privilege which remained to them was to leave the whirlpool of the ghetto for a quiet Catholic cemetery on the Aryan side.

10. The Doctor

WHENEVER I REMEMBER 33, Chlodna Street, which I do often, one man always comes to mind. Though I knew him for less than a year, I regarded him as a very close friend and I can never forget him. His name was Dr. Korman; before the war he had been a well-known paediatrician in Warsaw. He was politically left-wing and sympathised with the *Bund*, the Jewish secular socialist movement founded in Vilna in 1897. He and his wife came to live at number 33, while their only daughter and her husband, Dr. Herman, were somewhere in Russia.

Dr. Korman was a sensitive man and an idealist; the daily deterioration of our conditions in the ghetto affected him sadly. He was completely bewildered by the disintegration around him, and always looked to the house tenants for moral support. He often visited Dr. Korczak's orphanage, for the two men had much in common, professionally and otherwise; he also came frequently to us, and loved to talk about the pre-war world, the vanished world that had become as hazy as a dream. Because of his great love for Jewish tradition and customs, he always conversed with me in Yiddish. He invariably called on the Sabbath and festival days and was delighted to be invited by Janusz Korczak to a Passover evening.

It is interesting to note that life had become very cheap in the ghetto. This is an unusual attitude for those of the Jewish faith, but death was so common, so expected, that even the passing of a child seldom evoked comment or compassion. This attitude was transmitted even to the medical men, whose task was so hopeless that sympathy evaporated in the face of disease and death. And yet, in the moments of greatest horror, there were doctors who went on believing that their duty was to strive and to save. One of this devoted band was Dr. Korman. I often furnished him with lists of people who were sick and too poor to pay a doctor, and he went fearlessly from house to house trying to help and cure. Of course many of his patients died, but he never stopped working. Every evening he would tell me about his visits and give me a resumé of the state of his patients.

One day Dr. Korman came to tell me that he and his wife were leaving the ghetto. This was in the autumn of 1941. The Judenrat had suggested to him that, as a doctor, he could go to Zaklikow near Lublin. The Jews there were having a bad time; they were succumbing to sickness and were terribly short of medical aid. Dr. Korman said he had accepted this proposal for two reasons. First, a doctor *must* accede to this sort of request, and second, he hoped that in a small town it might be easier to survive, since he would not be incarcerated in a ghetto. The ghetto was suffocating; no fresh air, no trees, no grass. A small town was sure to be different; at least the air was unrationed. He also felt sure that my wife and I could find some opportunity of going to Zaklikow and staying there till the war ended. I thought the idea a good one and naïvely hoped that this would be a happy change of circumstances for us all. We decided that Dr. Korman and his wife would leave straight away, investigate conditions in the town and write and tell us when to come.

Every day we waited for a letter. Two weeks passed and we heard nothing; then some relations of his came to see us with sad news. Dr. Korman and his wife had arrived safely, but he had then contracted typhus and died suddenly. His wife was now trying to return to Warsaw. Weeks later I got a card from Korman himself, sent before he became ill. He described the desperate conditions in the town but said he was determined to stay and help. He warned us not to come.

I carried the card around with me for a long time, thinking it was an important piece of written evidence about this period of the war. I had it with me till the Polish Uprising of 1944. When I left the Old City through the sewers, I had many documents on me, including this card, but I had to discard all my possessions, so the card was lost for ever in the subterranean mire.

11. The Story of a Playground

IT WAS THE SPRING OF 1942. Everyone was afraid and rumours were spreading. As yet, Treblinka was unknown to us. We thought of the tragic events at Chelmno, Lublin, Vilna and other parts of Poland. The killing of thousands of Jews there was the topic of the day. In Warsaw itself, the silent streets of the ghetto at night could tell tales worthy of Dante's Inferno; people were dragged from their beds to be shot in the courtyards of their homes.

Nevertheless, we intended to open a playground for the children who attended the legal Jewish schools. This was to be the one happy event in our lives. There was a patch of vacant ground in Grzybowska Street where two houses had been bombed in September, 1939. This ground was opposite the offices of the Judenrat and the German authorities had permitted its conversion into a playground for the children of the ghetto. The ground was flattened and replanted with turf, fountains were erected and the remaining sections of wall were covered with bright murals representing Jewish themes. It was a symphony of colour.

It was decided to celebrate the opening of the playground on Lag B'Omer,* May 1942. Representatives of many cultural and social organisations were invited. There were about five hundred people in all, among them Rabbis, writers, educationists and former political leaders of the left and right. Thousands of children came, dressed in their best clothes and led by their teachers, and waited in groups for their previously-organised parade to begin. The members of the Judenrat assembled on a raised platform, waiting for the chairman, Adam Czerniakow. He and his group were the most important people invited, since the playground was their idea and they had paid for it.

The sun shone warmly and the orchestra of the Jewish Police Force played military music. Suddenly everyone was silent, and heads were turned towards the main entrance. Adam Czerniakow and his wife appeared. He wore a light tropical suit and a sun helmet. The orchestra struck up again. They walked towards the platform, surrounded by senior police officers; everybody got up when they reached the platform and the Jewish National Hymn was played.

When all the guests were seated, Adam Czerniakow opened the proceedings. His speech was brief and moving.

> These are tragic times, but we must stand firm. It is surely more than coincidence that the playground should be opposite the community centre. Whenever we hear children laughing and singing our windows will be open to let in the sound. This will give us hope and courage to go and fight for the future.

* A minor Jewish festival occurring between Passover and the wheat harvest festival Shavuoth.

He added that a new training college for teachers was to be opened, and also a ballet school for girls.

Many of the guests were critical of this ceremony. It was an open secret that we were on the edge of an abyss. Tragedy lay thick around us and this was hardly a suitable time for any sort of celebration. Janusz Korczak whispered in my ear, *"A Purim Spiel. . . ."*

The children filed past Adam Czerniakow, marching in time to the music, all heads turned towards the platform as they reached it. Later on they gave gymnastic displays to music.

Although this may not really have been the most propitious time for such festivity, the majority of people were impressed with the ceremony and the playground was now officially open for all the schoolchildren. A similar playground was later opened in the ghetto at the corner of Nalewki Street and Franciscan Street.

The days flew past and we were soon to reach the end of the academic school year at the end of June. How was one to celebrate this? It would have been simple for each school to have separate festivities on its own premises. But Czerniakow and his colleagues were determined to have a big joint celebration, as had always been the custom; so it was decided that all the schools should take part in a display in the new playground, at the beginning of July 1942, in the "Three Weeks"* period.

We were supposed to rehearse the children but there was no enthusiasm. Whispers had gone the rounds about the deportation of certain Jews from Warsaw. The Judenrat had provided identity cards for all their employees, intended to save them from deportation. As this had been authorised by the Germans they felt safe and in a position to continue organising some kind of celebration for the children; they also felt in the Judenrat that they must continue to behave as normally as possible, whatever happened. It seemed that we would have to proceed against our better judgement.

The time of celebration drew closer, each day punctuated by tragic events in Warsaw and elsewhere. I communicated with the heads of other schools—with Smolar, Majewski, Orlean, Friedenberg

* The time of mourning for the destruction of the Temple in Jerusalem by the Romans in A.D. 70.

and others. No one wanted any kind of ceremony, but no one dared disobey the Judenrat. We called a secret meeting in an attempt to find a way out of this impasse. Orlean had a good idea; he felt that the religious schools at least could not take part as this was the period of the "Three Weeks", and therefore a time of mourning. Surely this would be appreciated by the Judenrat?

The celebrations took place, but without the representatives of the religious schools. The members of the Judenrat were annoyed and ordered the heads of the schools to appear before a disciplinary committee. Surprisingly, only two headmasters were accused of not obeying orders—Orlean and Zylberberg. The committee consisted of the director of the Educational Department of the Judenrat, Abraham Wolfowicz; the secretary, Horenstein; and Dr. Tauber, the former principal of the Teachers' Training College in Warsaw. They harangued us for over two hours. The whole thing was unpleasant, especially as we were all old friends and it was difficult to be official. On the committee side, Mr. Horenstein was the most vocal. He argued that, in such desperate times, each one should try to compromise for the good of the community. Our defence, that we represented the religious element in teaching and so could not compromise, elicited the reply that under the present circumstances religion was no excuse, that orders should be obeyed. Mr. Orlean humorously remarked that we were still among friends and the Judenrat was not Gestapo headquarters. It was getting late and another meeting was suggested to determine the outcome.

Three days later, on 22nd July 1942, we saw the start of the tragic deportation to Treblinka. We did not meet the disciplinary committee again. These trifles were superseded by far graver problems.

12. Faith

IT IS SPRING, 1943. I have now been acting the part of a Catholic among Catholics for a number of months. Unwittingly one grows further and further away from one's previous environment. It is interesting, however, that right now I see in my mind's eye all the Jewish characters of former times. Particularly the religious Jews, who, till the last, believed that there was some order, some pattern in life, that everything was not chaos. They felt there was a deep meaning in their suffering and death which would be perpetuated in Jewish history. These people seem more real to me every day. I feel that they accompany me wherever I go, indoors and out, even to the church which I visit so frequently.

Of course any religious Jew who saw the sufferings of his people was tormented by doubts. He saw the sorrows of the children and the old and the ill constantly around him. Often, in this nightmare, one felt this to be a world of neither laws nor judges, and one often felt compelled to ask one's self, "We lived by the Torah, and is this the reward?" The religious Jews tried to dispel their doubts by strengthening their beliefs, which were even stronger, perhaps, than in pre-war years. The Yeshivot were full to overflowing with eager students at that time.

As the situation deteriorated daily, so the religious Jews sought hope in the supernatural, turning to a new cabbalistic* interpretation of words from which a shred of comfort might be drawn. This tendency had begun in 1941 and the tortured searchings were even more intense in 1942. For example: a Rabbi reinterpreted the quotation, "When the Sabbath comes it brings with it peace". The Hebrew letters are used as numbers and the letters of the word Sabbath are 702. In the Hebrew calendar the year 702 coincides with 1942. This, they said, would be a year of peace, this year would see the end of the war. The extermination programme started in that year.

I often had to visit the Gerer Rabbi's† grandchild, Rabbi Naphtali, in Twarda Street, and his brother in Muranov Street. They both accepted the tragedy philosophically. They sat self-contained, quiet and impassive, showing neither fear nor capitulation. They seemed almost to accept their fate as a punishment, not of Divine

* *Cabbala*—the major work of medieval Jewish mysticism.

† Prominent Chassidic dynasty of Rabbis of the Alter family whose residence was in the town of Ger (Góra Kalvaria), near Warsaw.

but of human origin, because society had allowed barbaric men to rule the world. In the early days of the deportations the Gerer Rabbi's brother once appeared in the street. He ran quickly towards a street in which people were being arrested by the Germans. I shouted at him to warn him of the danger and begged him to go home. He did not seem to recognize me. He looked at me in a bewildered manner, but remained silent. The sorrow of previous generations of Jews spoke through his eyes.

When, in the spring of 1942, we started to hear terrible reports from the countryside, a student from the Gostynin Yeshiva came to Warsaw with a letter to the Rabbis. It came from his colleagues. They asked whether they should escape and hide in the nearby woods. The answer was that all the young people should leave the town, and, though it was dangerous, should hide out in the forest. They were warned to be careful of attracting too much attention as the majority of the Jews had to stay put.

In the early days of the catastrophe, at the end of July 1942, we usually stayed in the Jewish community archive office in Grzybowska Street. We thought and hoped that this building would protect us. In one corner of the archive room sat a famous elderly Rabbi, Rabbi Kanal, always with his prayer book and reciting psalms. He avoided human contact and talked to no one. When he was once asked what fate had in store, he said quietly, "So many Jews have died in God's name that one more old man can make no difference." A few days later he faced the Germans, refusing to get into the train which was transporting the Jews to Treblinka. He was shot then and there.

It is difficult to forget something which happened at the end of 1942. It was bitterly cold in the offices of the Judenrat building in Zamenhof Street. Some people were sitting in one of the rooms, most of them religious. Among them was Professor Mayer Balaban. People talked of the day's events and the uncertainties of tomorrow, but the professor sat silent. One of the group, Jehuda Orlean, the well-known educationist and Aguda leader, said he avoided religious services as he did not want to be questioned. He had no comforting answers to give. Also, he did not want people to see him without a beard. Rabbi Schreibman, on the other hand, said that this was the time to tell people that it was not the end. Times were bad, but one must have faith and not despair. Without faith there could be no life. I heard him say the same thing a few days later at a wedding. In the few months before the total destruction of the ghetto there were many marriages between young couples recently bereaved. They would ask the Rabbi for words of hope, and Rabbi Schreibman would repeat his comforting message.

On another occasion, when the Orthodox leader Isaac Ber Eckerman was present, we discussed the tragedy again. Eckerman asked about some of his friends, and when he was told that they had already disappeared, he called out, "No one is left. This is our fate; not one of us will survive." Another Rabbi in the room answered, "Is survival important? One thing matters—the defeat of the enemy. You must surely believe this. Their defeat is so certain that this must be our comfort."

On Rosh Hashana, 1942, after a massive selection of victims in the ghetto, everyone felt extremely ill at ease. No one knew if the selection—which had started some days previously—had come to an end. People crept out of hiding and asked each other, "What is happening in the streets?" The streets were empty and silent. Suddenly a Jew appeared complete with beard and side-curls, accompanied by an exhausted woman. Both of them could hardly totter. They were covered with feathers and had obviously just crept out of a mountain of bedclothes where they had been hiding. The man kept raising his clenched fists to heaven and the poor woman who led him wept uncontrollably and shouted, "My husband has gone mad." "Jews," he called, "collect large stones and throw them up to heaven! Why has God picked on us for this torment? Give me stones to throw in defiance of heaven!" His wife was shocked at the blasphemy and tried to apologise for him, saying, "He has had neither food nor water for days. He is terrified. He is not responsible for what he is saying." The scene spelt the disintegration of a deep religious faith.

Many months have separated me from that scene, but I always hear the cry, "Stones, collect stones!"

13. Reb Zishe and Reb Zalman

FATE HAD DRIVEN THEM TO WARSAW at the very beginning of
the war: Reb Zishe from Mlava, a disciple of the Gerer Rabbi, a
scholar and a sage, and Reb Zalman from Bialystock, a follower
of the Lubavitch Rabbi, a man of transparent honesty, his sincere
goodness reflected in his patriarchal dignity. Reb Zishe was nearly
eighty, well-preserved, agile and humorous. He believed that Jews
were never forsaken and would not be conquered. Reb Zalman
was younger, about seventy, moving with effort, filled with hope,
taking all that happened as Divine punishment.

Both Reb Zishe and Reb Zalman settled with their wives in one
room at number 21 Franciscan Street. The room was partitioned
with a sheet, as often happened in a poor one-room hut when
childbirth was imminent. Although they had departed in haste
from their homes, they brought with them all the possessions that
were for them both sacred and important. Reb Zishe had with
him his fur-trimmed *shtreiml*,* his silk caftan, his silver candlesticks, his silver goblet and, above all, his sacred books. His small
table was always covered with books. They were his whole world
now.

Reb Zalman's half of the room looked very much the same. He
too had brought his books, his most important possessions. On
his table was displayed the *Tanya*, the book written by the first
Lubavitch Rabbi.

The families lived in harmony in spite of their cramped quarters.
The women made every effort to keep their husbands fed. They
were not really short of money at first as they had formerly been
businessmen, had owned their own houses, and had enjoyed a
reasonable income. For Reb Zalman, if the truth be known, the
habits and way of life of Reb Zishe, a Gerer disciple, appeared
rather odd. He nevertheless treated him with great respect. Both

* Headgear worn by Orthodox Jews in Eastern Europe.

of them, however, maintained the same religious standards that they had cherished before the war. Illegal religious services were held in the private rooms of the house and there was also a ritual bath. It all seemed so familiar at first. Of course times were hard and no day was without its tragedy. But they lived in hope. God would surely help them.

When the Sabbath arrived all was warmth and light: Reb Zishe in his *shtreiml* and his silk caftan, Reb Zalman in his Sabbath clothes, and the candlesticks on the white tablecloths adding their own lustre. We have to admit that the tables here were rather more frugal than the normal Sabbath tables. No fish, no meat; nevertheless the proper sentiments prevailed and the day was helped along with religious songs. They were both tolerant men and tried not to disturb each other, since their songs were different. One deferred to the other and, in fact, they sang in sequence. The room was open house for every neighbour. Reb Zishe was a good conversationalist and it was a joy for anyone to have an hour's chat with him. Many people from his home town came to see him, some of them far from religious. They all seemed to regain hope after talking to him. Reb Zalman sat apart, listening and smiling. He was supremely happy to hear the wit, the encouraging remarks and the religious quotations of his neighbour. This was how the days and months passed. The courtyard of the house seemed like a miniature town with all its varied activities, and all that happened there was seen by these two religious men, who sat looking out of the window.

Then Reb Zalman became restless. He wanted Reb Zishe to explain to him what was actually happening in the world. When Reb Zalman saw the anguish of parents with hungry children, when he saw children dying of hunger in the courtyard, he was overcome with sadness. He could not sleep at night but tossed and turned and groaned and questioned, "What is happening? Children die of starvation, innocent young people are being shot. What has happened to the world, Reb Zishe? What about the Biblical saying, 'Each man dies for his sins'? Have these children sinned?"

But Reb Zishe had always only one reply, "Go back to sleep, Reb Zalman. Don't ask questions."

This did not satisfy the old man. He wanted in his innocence to know what had happened to the world, what this sort of behaviour meant.

The extermination programme was drawing closer. Life became harder every day and the scenes in the courtyard were indescribable. Each day was more tragic than the one before. Reb Zishe held firm to his faith. Reb Zalman, a gentler man, was utterly lost in a sea of murder. He clung to his neighbour and they hid together during the German searches. Reb Zalman regarded his friend as a tower of strength, for without him he would surely have died long before.

The High Holydays were approaching. Reb Zishe, Reb Zalman and their wives were still together. They ran from cellar to cellar, from attic to attic, and to other hiding places. It was a cat and mouse game. Reb Zalman did not move without Reb Zishe. Both tried to live as they had always done, praying three times a day, and both were fully prepared to die in the name of God. Reb Zalman was still trying to understand, to find the meaning of what was happening. He was more troubled than ever by the cruel fate of the children. One day, when he could no longer stand upright because of the effects of starvation, Reb Zalman put the question which had troubled him for so long, *"Zu Torah Ve'zu Secharah?*—We Lived by the Torah; is this the reward?"* He waited for an answer from Reb Zishe. Reb Zishe turned pale, looked harshly at his friend and said, "You sin, Reb Zalman; we must never lose hope."

The tie between the two men persisted. They were inseparable till the last day. On the eve of the Day of Atonement the house was surrounded by the Germans and there was no escape. Reb Zishe, calm as ever, asked Reb Zalman, "Have you got your *tallis?*★ Have you got your *kittel?"*† Reb Zalman answered in a shaky voice and took Reb Zishe by the hand, and they and their wives left the cruel world. They must have arrived at the Throne of Heaven in time for the solemn Kol-Nidre service.

★ Woollen prayer shawl.
† A traditional garment worn by Jewish men on Yom Kippur; they are finally buried in it.

The synagogues and prayer houses in Warsaw are now empty, dark and sad. No traditional candles, no chanting, no prayers. The crowds of men, women and children are now assembled in Heaven. Among them are our two religious men, Reb Zalman and Reb Zishe. The crowds neither pray nor move—they are stunned into horrified silence. Suddenly Reb Zalman starts moving forward, pushing his way through the crowd. He is now less in awe of his old friend Reb Zishe. At the foot of the Throne his cry breaks the silence,

> *Zu Torah Ve'zu Secharah?*
> We Lived By The Torah; is this The reward?

The echo reverberates through the Halls of Heaven. There is no answer.

Living now in a new world, disguised as a Pole and a Catholic, I often think of those people, of whom not even a handful could be saved. The religious ones inhabited a world of their own, and a few had friends among the Poles, who might have saved them. Few of them knew Polish well enough to be able to escape detection in Polish society. And their unique way of life also segregated them so completely that they all, hundreds of thousands of them, vanished in the smoke of the many extermination camps.

Added in London

Among the survivors I interviewed in recent years in London was a man who survived seventeen days in Treblinka. It is interesting to record some of the words of this witness in the light of Orthodox Jewish belief.

A trainload containing thousands of victims arrived from Warsaw on the morning of the first day of Rosh Hashana. Among them were three Rabbis, Rabbi Srebrnik from Zakroczym, his son, Rabbi Srebrnik from Brodnice, and Rabbi Borenstein from Plonsk. The Germans ordered the men to undress in the open. They then stood naked, awaiting their fate. Standing there, bewildered, awaiting death, one of the Rabbis said, "It is Rosh Hashana, and we should pray now." Many of the naked Jews took

up their prayer shawls, and started chanting. This, to a certain
extent, had a calming effect. They were soon hurried on, however, and in this manner they all entered the gas chamber. All,
that is, except the narrator, who miraculously met his brother.
The brother's job was to collect the discarded clothes, and he
pulled the intended victim into the group of workers.

How much spiritual strength was required to pray like this in
the face of death?

14. Songs of Praise

IT WAS THE END OF JUNE, 1942. People were becoming progres-
sively more demoralised. News of the mass slaughter of Jews in
the provinces was reaching us more and more frequently. Warsaw
itself had become a sort of playground for the Germans; they
picked out people at random, day and night, and murdered them
in cold blood. One got the impression that the Germans wanted to
provoke the Jews into "subversive" activity. In the last weeks
before the deportations, for no reason at all, they had shot one
hundred and ten men and women and had put up posters saying
that this was a reprisal for the killing of a few Germans. Everyone
knew that this was untrue. Nevertheless, the Jews were still well-
disciplined and courageous.

In this atmosphere of terror we decided to end the school year
with a solemn service for the children. It took place two weeks
before the final holocaust, on a Saturday morning at the Moriah
Synagogue in Dzielna Street, and was conducted by the children
themselves. There was a choir of young infants and in all about a
thousand children took part. Before the war the synagogue had
been the centre of Zionist sympathies and preaching, and during
the war years it was a shelter and home for those Jews sent to the
ghetto from the provinces. For this one Saturday the Judenrat had
asked these people to vacate the building and they sent a group of
their own representatives to attend the service.

It started at nine, but at eight one could already see many children, led by their teachers, converging on the synagogue from several streets. Hundreds of boys and girls, between seven and sixteen, dressed in their best clothes. Everybody was cheerful. It was hard to believe, looking at them, that despair and starvation were encircling us, and that epidemics were claiming hundreds of victims every day. They looked so remote from terror and danger. Those children were a credit to parents who had done all they could to make them look happy and human; they had demonstrated the triumph of their hope.

In the synagogue the children separated; the girls went up into the women's gallery, and the boys stayed in the body of the hall. They were very much in charge, this Sabbath.

The service started with a poem sung by the choir of a thousand children in honour of the Sabbath; its author was one of the teachers, a man called Gothart. It was followed by the solemn service, the boys acting as cantors. This was easy for them, as they were taught in Hebrew at school and could read and sing the prayers without difficulty, obviously understanding every word. They also read the appropriate portion of the Law and called forward their teachers and the representatives of various institutions to utter the benedictions, thus showing them esteem and respect. The service was outstanding for the quality of the singing, which had been carefully rehearsed. The songs in praise of the Sabbath, with their famous liturgical tunes, were rendered with special clarity. The echo of these treble voices singing in a Warsaw synagogue for the last time will always be with me.

There was neither preacher nor sermon, but two longings could be distinctly felt—the yearning for freedom and the urge to go to the land of Israel. The final song, in which everybody joined, was the Jewish national hymn *Hatikva*, and both desires are expressed there.

Dr. Tauber of the Judenrat, when he thanked the children, stressed that the proceedings had taken place unofficially, since services were not allowed in the ghetto and speeches, in particular, were definitely forbidden. But he was glad it had all happened. He remarked ironically that being alive was also illegal in the ghetto—

yet we still survived. The preacher of the synagogue, Rabbi Nissenbaum, who had been there for many years, did not take part. He was a very old man and his sight was failing. It was, in fact, dangerous for him to go out into the street as he could hardly see at all. So, on that same day, we went and told him all about the children's service in great detail. It moved him deeply and it was probably the last piece of good news he ever received, for he died shortly afterwards at Treblinka.

Who knows if any of those children survived?

15. Remembering Herzl and Bialik

ONLY A FEW DAYS lay between us and the beginning of the extermination programme which spelled the end of the largest Jewish community in Europe. We were tormented by conflicting rumours of death and deportation; one tale contradicted the next. Terror mounted and night and day merged in wakefulness. Was it possible to think seriously of holding a commemoration day for two national figures, Theodor Herzl and Chaim Nahman Bialik? Before the war mass meetings of Zionists were held everywhere on the anniversary of their deaths. This had become a custom in the 1930's, for the founder of Zionism and the national Hebrew poet were held in great reverence by Polish Jews, particularly the young ones. They saw in the ideas of Herzl and the writings of Bialik a realisation of their hopes. They were commemorated on the same day.

The time of the meeting was unobtrusively fixed. It was to be at four in the afternoon, at the Artists' and Authors' Club in Orla Street. I was secretly informed of this by an author called Berenstein, Abraham Chanachowitch, a young journalist, and the writer Berenholz-Selim, who had managed to get back into the ghetto from Soviet-occupied territory. I was determined to attend, whatever the risk. And so, silently, I joined the many well-known people who crept into the club house. Apart from

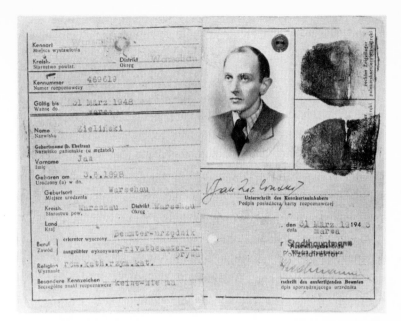

The author's identity card (*Kennkarte*) in the name of Jan Zielinski, a Polish Catholic

Identity card of the author's wife, Henrietta, in the name of a Polish Catholic

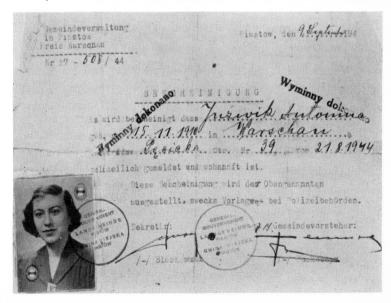

Aufruf

An die Einwohner des jüdischen Wohnbezirks.

Gemäss Anordnung der Behörden vom 22. Juli 1942 werden alle Personen, welche nicht in Anstalten und Unternehmen tätig sind, unbedingt umgesiedelt.

Die Zwangsaussiedlung wird ununterbrochen weitergeführt. Ich fordere erneut die der Aussiedlung unterliegende Bevölkerung auf, sich freiwillig auf dem Umschlagplatz zu melden und verlängere auf weitere 3 Tage, d. h. den 2., 3. und 4. August 1942 die Ausgabe von 3 kg. Brot und 1 kg. Marmelade an jede sich freiwillig meldende Person.

Freiwillig zur Abreise erscheinende Familien werden nicht getrennt.

Sammelpunkt für Freiwillige: Dzika 3 – Stawki 27.

Der Leiter des Ordnungsdienstes

Warschau, den 1. August 1942

Notice calling on Jews to report for deportation, August 1942

Chlodna Bridge, which divided the large ghetto from the small. The author lived at Chlodna 17 (see page 68) in the block of flats shown here

Zionist leaders, there were also people who would normally never have come. They were about a hundred in all, trying to hide their secret worry about a sudden German raid on the house. Everyone waited. The platform was bare, and there was no sign of the organisers.

At four o'clock exactly, Rabbi Jechiel Mayer Blumenfeld stood up amongst the assembled group, approached the rostrum, mounted, and turned to look at the audience. In a few brief moments he expressed what we all felt.

"Herzl was not brought up in the Jewish tradition, but he returned to Judaism because he saw the horrors in store for European Jews. He knew that antisemitism was a potent source of danger.

"Bialik also, in his poems, has recorded for eternity the pogroms against Jews. The pogrom in Kishiniev in 1904 inspired him to write a poem, and on the tombstone of the Kishiniev victims is written, at his request: 'May the earth never cover their blood'. Undoubtedly we should now, in these tragic days, remember those great men on the anniversary of their deaths."

We were deeply moved when the Rabbi referred to the slaughter of Jews in Vilna, Lublin and other towns. We shuddered, though the facts had been long known to us.

Rabbi Blumenfeld ended with the hope that some miracle would happen to free us from German domination. He stepped off the platform and sat down amongst the audience. After a few minutes' silence, the actor Jacques Levy went on stage and recited Bialik's poem *Al Ha' Shechita*—"On the Slaughter". It seemed as if a whole nation were reciting the impassioned words. The audience shivered.

> Heavens! Entreat for mercy in my name,
> If there's a God in you, and to that God
> A road I have not found—
> Speak prayers in my name!
> My heart is dead, upon my lips no song
> Of prayer; strength has failed, hope is no more—
> How long, till when, how long?
> Headsman! Here is my neck—come, strike it through!

Neck me like a dog, the axe is in your hand,
And all the world's my block—
And we—why, we are few!
My blood is gratis—smite, let flow the gore,
The blood of babes and greybeards stains your coat—
'Twill never be wiped o'er.
If there is Right, then let it now be shown!
For if when I have perished 'neath the skies
The Right shine forth, I pray
Crushed over be its throne!
And through eternal wrong the heavens shall wilt;
But walk, ye recreants, in your violence;
Live in your blood sans guilt.

Cursed be the man who cries, "Vengeance for this".
Vengeance for this—the blood of little children—
The devil has not framed.
The blood will pierce the abyss,
To the gloomy depths the blood will worm its way,
Devour in darkness, gnaw upon the earth's
Foundations in decay.*

When he had ended he also stepped down amongst the people.
A violinist then played Acharon's "Melodies" and the meeting
ended; the whole thing had lasted half an hour. As we were
leaving Yitzhak Schiper, the historian, praised the Rabbi for his
brave words. He also marvelled at his appearance. The Rabbi had
worn a short alpaca coat and highly polished shoes. This was his
personal form of resistance to the degradation around him, since
many others had become neglectful of their persons. Dr. Schiper
was among the few who, like the Rabbi, were careful of their
dress and general appearance until the end.

Yechiel Mayer Blumenfeld had a distinguished life and a tragic
death. Before the war he had been a lecturer in Rabbinics at the
Seminary in Warsaw, and was one of the leaders of the Mizrachi
(religious Zionist) movement. In the ghetto he was chairman of
the Association of Rabbis (a group comprising a few hundred
members). He was always anxious to offer help, especially to those

* *Writings of Chaim Nahman Bialik*, Berlin, 1923. This poem was translated
by L. V. Snowman.

Rabbis who had been forcibly sent to Warsaw from other towns and countries. In 1941 he succeeded in contacting some Jewish organisations in neutral countries and sent them a list of Rabbis in the ghetto; they received food parcels for some time as a result of this intercession. When the extermination began in July, 1942, Rabbi Blumenfeld worked in a factory to escape deportation. It belonged to the brothers Landau, who were well-known Zionists, and they hoped that by employing many writers, Rabbis and teachers as factory workers they could save their lives.

One day the SS arrived at the factory saying they needed healthy young men for work at Smolensk. Not many people were anxious to go; they realised that this was a trick to get rid of those who might still rebel against them. Nevertheless, some of them were forcibly rounded up, among them Rabbi Blumenfeld. He thought that, being over fifty, he would not have to go to Smolensk, so he approached one of the Germans and showed his identity card which stated his age. The officer took out his pistol and shot the Rabbi repeatedly through the head. When the body fell covered with blood, the officer kicked it aside shouting, *"Die Bestie blutigt"*. This event was witnessed and told to me on the same day by a relation of mine, who worked in the same factory.

The young people who were rounded up were sent to Treblinka that very evening.

16. Round-up in Zamenhof Street

It was August, 1942, and the rounding-up of victims had been going on for twelve days. The Jewish police were still active in assisting the Germans to carry out the operation. The Germans themselves often made spot raids in the ghetto and vacated whole blocks of their inhabitants for deportation. They were not always seen in the streets, but were very much in charge at the station (the *Umschlagplatz*) to which victims were brought to be packed onto trains. At this time the name "Treblinka" was still unknown in the ghetto, although many people knew that deportation meant certain death.

My wife and I now lived at 17, Chlodna Street. We, like every-one else, hid in the cellars, since we knew about the raids in the street. They usually started at about six in the morning and went on till noon. In the afternoon I used to leave the house to find out what had happened. Number seventeen was close to the foot-bridge over Chlodna Street which linked both sides of the ghetto; in fact, there was a smaller and a larger ghetto. Not far away lived many Judenrat officials and officers of the Jewish police. Adam Czerniakow was also a near neighbour at 20, Chlodna Street. It was a district where, because of its special class of residents, one could usually find people walking in the streets, so I approached a passer-by and asked if today's deportation snatch was finished. The man assured me that the ghetto was quiet. The Germans had asked for six thousand people and that number had been supplied.

In those days we were still thinking and reacting normally and making plans; for example, how to avoid being deported. We deluded ourselves into believing that in a few more days all would be well. I was busy thinking about my work as a headmaster, mentally preparing a syllabus for the new autumn term. I decided, therefore, to take the opportunity of visiting the school secretary, Schulim Rosenbaum, who lived at 24, Zamenhof Street, and together we would arrange the timetable for the coming year. This had to be presented to the Judenrat's Department of Education. I went back to tell my wife where I was going, promising to be back before dark. The streets were a hive of activity—a sign that the raids were temporarily over. During the raids, there was never a soul to be seen. I walked to the place where the secretary lived. He and his wife and child occupied one room of a two-roomed flat which belonged to a Chassidic family. The owner himself was ill in bed and lay there reciting psalms. As soon as I entered everybody asked for news and they were glad to learn that the danger was over for the day.

We sat down at the table and started work. We talked, how-ever, about events in the ghetto. Schulim, who was an enthusiastic youth leader, reminded me of the last Zionist Congress in Geneva;

he had returned from there on the day war broke out. At the time, he was delighted to get back to his wife and child. What would they have done without him?

Suddenly we heard running feet in the courtyard. Looking out of the window, we saw people scurrying about, frightened and bewildered. In a few moments the courtyard was full of German officers. They shouted that all the inhabitants of the block should come down to the street at once; anyone staying indoors would be shot. My first question was—is there a hiding place here? Rosenbaum and his wife looked at me in amazement. They said, "We are properly employed and have cards issued by the Judenrat to prove it." The cards were also stamped with the words, *Unterliegt nicht der Umsiedlung*—"Not subject to deportation". I felt claustrophobic; the end seemed close. I had never believed in official papers and certainly not in generous exceptions on the part of the Germans.

In a few minutes we were in the street, amongst the thousands already there. There were men, women and children. On each side German soldiers, Ukrainians and Lithuanians* were standing guard over the silent, motionless crowd. Many of the Jews were clad only in undergarments, having come straight from their sick beds. Among them was the Chassidic owner of the secretary's flat.

At the corner of Gensia Street and Zamenhof Street stood two elegantly turned-out German officers, accompanied by the Jewish police officer Sherynski, while their black limousine was parked on Gensia Street. Both Germans, smoking cigars, were looking through the identity cards and standing to face their victims, who surged towards them. They had to make snap decisions—whether one went to the left or to the right. Nearly everyone was sent to the left—for deportation. A few minutes—and we were in front of the officers. They looked at our identity cards and proclaimed "Left!" I joined the crowd with Rosenbaum and his wife and child, well-guarded by the black-uniformed aides.

As we stood there, terror and a desperate sense of danger overwhelmed us with stark reality. At that instant a Jewish policeman

* The Germans enlisted special units of Ukrainians, Lithuanians and Latvians to assist in the destruction of the Jews.

passed by. I tried to give him all my personal possessions, my watch and my money, and begged him to save us. He said, "At this stage, there is nothing that the Jewish police can do. They, the Germans, are the ones who make the final decisions. Anyway, an empty train is waiting for you at the station." Usually the victims waited one or two days at the station before they boarded the train.

Each minute seemed eternity. I knew that my wife was sitting and waiting at home—while I stood on the verge of death. Now other people were joining us and I whispered to Rosenbaum, "Move to the back of the crowd. Perhaps some miracle will happen." One of the German officers came up to the guard and asked how many of us there were. As soon as he had been told, he asked for the group to be taken to the station. Crying out, "Faster! Faster!", the Germans marched us to the *Umschlagplatz* about ten minutes away. The Rosenbaums and I tried to keep to the rear of the group all the time, while the Ukrainians pushed us forward with their rifle butts, realising full well what we were trying to do. The Jewish policeman was right; the train was there and waiting. Here, looking at the train and along the platform, we saw the whole pattern of destruction. There were dead and injured bodies lying around and the living victims were being hastily pushed into the carriages.

Frienziedly, I was making plans to escape. In a second I had whipped off the belt from my trousers, buckled it tightly round my jacket, and turned round to face a German officer at the edge of the crowd. I stood to attention, saluted smartly and said, "Sir, I have brought 500 more." He looked at me and pushed me back with his pistol. I realised I had violated military discipline—I should have stood three paces from him. I stepped back, saluted again and repeated the sentence. He smiled and said, "*Jude, mach los*—Jew, go back." My sudden action at that psychological moment had convinced him I was one of the Jewish police. But I had come with my friend and his wife and child. I looked around. He was already inside the train but I saw her standing, holding the child. I turned again, saluted the German and said, "Sir, my wife and child are here." I pointed to them. The German went over, pushed them towards me and said, "Here is your wife and child, Jew, go back." We walked wordless to the gate at the end of the platform. The guards who had witnessed the scene stepped back to let us pass. I was free again, and had saved my friend's wife and child for the time being.

On the way back we were in danger again. A new group of victims was being led to the station and we might have been made to join them. Miraculously, we managed to slip into my school which was nearby in Kupiecka Street. Realisation dawned on the unhappy woman and she spilled out the whole story to the teachers who were in hiding in the school. I had managed to prolong her life, but only for a few months. In January, 1943, she and her child and thousands of others were deported.

I got home at dusk. My wife was waiting, anxious and upset. How could a visit to Zamenhof Street have taken so long? I made up my mind to tell her nothing.

17. The "Selection"

IT ALL BEGAN AT NIGHT, at a time when the midnight service before Rosh Hashana would normally have been held. Regardless of the fact that after curfew no one was allowed out, people were rushing around the courtyard. You could hear the main entrance gate swinging open and footsteps passing in and out. These belonged to Jewish police bringing notice of a German order to all the tenants: On the following morning, Sunday, all Jews had to vacate their dwellings, and move into a few pre-arranged streets which were to comprise the new ghetto. Those refusing to leave would be shot.

No one really understood the order. Were the streets where we now lived really to be excluded from the ghetto? Or was this a new form of trickery, to make deportation to Treblinka easier?

We were now living at 9, Smocza Street; the street in which we had lived before had been excluded from the ghetto a few days previously. The order to move from there had come at dawn and we had to vacate within two hours. And now we were being asked to move again, a short distance, to Libelt Street. It was narrow and dirty and it was supposed to rehouse a few thousand people, all workers from the Hoffmann factory. It is ironic that this cramped alley had been named after a famous Polish revolutionary who fought for justice and independence.

The night was alive with activity. People scurried around, seeking advice from their neighbours. To add to the problem, there were no hiding-places in the block of flats, so to ignore the order meant certain death.

A relation of mine, Naphtali Zylberberg, lived in the same house at Smocza Street with his family. He was a journalist and always managed to keep well-informed about everything in the ghetto. I talked to him in the courtyard. Should we go or risk staying? We decided that in the morning we should leave. It was obvious to everyone that there was no point in taking belongings with us—they were no help against deportation. We also knew what happened to deportees. Treblinka was now a well-known word. And so, the following morning, we moved out, leaving everything behind and the doors of the house wide open for any-one to go in as he pleased. I had some money, but what use would that be in Treblinka? So I parcelled it up and put it in the bottom of the large communal dustbin, piling the refuse back on top.

We were engulfed by a mass of people, walking and pushing and shuffling from all sides into the new ghetto. The day was very hot, unbearably so, and the pressure of the crowd on all sides was suffocating. We saw friends and relations, all frightened and dis-tressed and wondering what was going to happen. I noticed in the crowd an old friend of mine, Gershon Fraenkel. Just before the war he had completed his Oriental studies in Belgium; now, he was hardly recognisable. His normally corpulent frame was emaciated; he was wearing two suits and a heavy winter top coat, not realising, apparently, that this was the heat of late summer. The perspiration was pouring down his face. I said to him, "Take some of those clothes off; you'll feel the better for it." We knew that people who looked ill, worried or mentally disturbed were the first to be rounded up for Treblinka. I never, in fact, saw him again.

Shortly afterwards, we arrived at the small street. People were begging for a drink of water and giving all they had for one sip. The directors of our factory immediately requisitioned a room as temporary premises and instructions passed by word of mouth that all the workers were to come and re-register. They had each had a factory number, but were now to have a new one. Then, the unbelievable horror—all those issued with new numbers, we heard, were going to be selected by the Germans. This was announced by the Jewish factory directors. We gazed around, panic-stricken, for a means of escape, but the street was surrounded by Germans and their Lithuanian aides. We had been tricked; it was all up with us.

I queued with the others and eventually managed to see the directors, who informed me that there was no number for my wife or for me. What could this mean? No number meant no work and hence, no chance of survival; non-producers went straight to Treblinka. I begged and shouted, to no avail. Then I suddenly thought of my relation Naphtali Zylberberg; perhaps he would help me. Someone said he had changed his mind at the last minute and had not come; so seeing him was out of the question. I was trapped. The streets around were heavily guarded.

Then, the sudden order: all those with new numbers were to go to the main street for selection, and the others were to stay in Libelt Street. At that last moment the directors relented and gave me Naphtali's number, which meant that I could go on to the main street, but my wife had to stay put.

In the main street, men and women were being separated into groups of one hundred strong. I said goodbye to my wife and tried to calm her, saying that we would be sure to meet after the selection. I set out to join the fifth group. As we stood there, we saw SS-men surrounding the crowd left without numbers, among whom was Henrietta. They began to shoot haphazardly into the crowd and we saw the dead and wounded fall. I acted on pure instinct; I ran from my group towards the numberless crowd and shouted my wife's name, Henrietta, at the top of my voice. She pushed herself forward at the sound of her name. A Ukrainian guard smiled at her, turned aside his machine-gun and allowed her to pass out to me. I took her back to my group and made her stand beside me—the only woman in a crowd of a hundred men. The others screamed at me. "You will now have us shot for certain, bringing a female here!" I tried to pacify them. We were interrupted by the Germans, who were ready to select victims.

They picked quite a few from the first group, among them the directors of the factory. It was obvious that the Germans were not interested in numbers. They treated the whole thing as a complete farce and simply selected those whose faces, for some reason or other, they did not like. The selectors drew nearer to the fifth group. There, in the front row, stood five men and one woman. None of us breathed. The Germans coolly looked us over—and passed by. The whole row was saved from deportation, Henrietta and I with them. Somehow, a miracle had happened, and the psychological causes were beyond analysis. People behind us were selected; some wore glasses, some carried packages, some were very old and others very young. Of the five thousand workers who had been in the factory the previous day, only five hundred were to return.

The group included a man from Pinsk, elderly and completely silent, whose name was Galperin. I saw that his wife had just joined him. Before the war he had been the wealthy director of a match factory. We had worked together in the ghetto factory and were also close neighbours in Smocza Street. He now looked completely lost; he stood and waited, not knowing what for. In response to the order, "*Raus*—out", he stepped forward, leaving his valise in the roadway. It probably contained a fortune in money and jewellery, but no one picked it up, though they knew what was in it.

I remember, too, the deaf-mute from Lodz. He had a child's perambulator filled with a selection of patent medicines and pills; by using sign language he sold just enough to buy bread for his wife and children. There he was, in one of the other groups, with his pram. The Germans mocked him, and made him scurry from one group to another; he, sallow and misshapen, had no grasp of what was happening and ran busily. The Germans laughed and he went with his pathetic little carriage to Treblinka. After we had been standing several hours, the Germans re-counted the five hundred left and told them to return to the factory in Smocza Street. All the others, with and without numbers, had been condemned to death. Henrietta and I were alive. It was September 6th, 1942.

18. Day of Atonement, 1942

AFTER ALL THE MONTHS of selections and round-ups, there were five hundred of us left in the SS-man Hoffmann's factory. We tried not to brood on all our tragic experiences and on our rapidly diminishing numbers, and some flicker of optimism sustained us. We all hoped that our small band of workers, now recognised as efficient, would manage to survive in the ghetto without further danger.

After the September selection, we realised with disquiet that the High Holydays were rapidly approaching. We knew that the Germans issued their extermination orders to coincide with the Jewish festivals; for example, we were ordered to form a ghetto during the Yom Kippur services of 1940. The first deportation order was issued to us on the 9th Av, the anniversary of the destruction of the Temple.

The two days of the New Year festival passed fairly quietly for us, in contrast to the other streets and factories, where life was unbearable. But for all of us, free movement in the streets was impossible, since the Germans were out on an orgy of shooting and killing. After work we would march as a group from the factory in Nowolipki Street to our homes in Smocza Street.

On the day before Yom Kippur we were suddenly told that we were free to leave work at midday. That seemed highly suspicious, but we went home and made feeble attempts to prepare for the occasion. We wanted to behave as normally as possible, as this sort of continuity gave us strength. Suddenly news reached us that the Germans were coming into our houses to carry out a new selection; we heard, also, that people without factory numbers would go straight to Treblinka. The main house-gate was locked and Jewish police stood on guard to see that no one attempted to escape. There was, of course, nowhere to escape to. It is hard to describe the feeling of tragedy which hung over the house. There were many people there who had no jobs or numbers, including my own wife, so there was only one thing to do—hide them in the attics, which had a trapdoor and a sliding ladder that they could drag up with them. But this evacuation had to take place speedily as the SS might be upon us at any moment. In a matter of seconds, twelve people were up in one of the attics, my wife among them. The ladder was drawn up and the trapdoor fastened. Now we could only pray that the Germans would not see the entrance to the hiding place. The SS arrived soon afterwards, and ordered everyone with numbers to assemble in the courtyard. Then they themselves went into the house searching for the so-called "illegal inhabitants".

Standing in the yard, we peered through the staircase windows and saw the Germans mounting up to the fourth floor. Now they were standing under the trapdoor. We heard them call out to the caretaker, "A ladder, please." I stood in the courtyard utterly shattered. It was all over. The caretaker, an engineer by profession, knew about the people in hiding and wanted to help. I ran up to him in the yard, begged him to take a long time searching for a ladder and pleaded, "Is there no way out?" He said, "The only way is to take a risk. There are two trapdoor entrances to the attic. The other is in a section of the house where there aren't any Germans. We can chance someone going up through the second trapdoor and getting those people out."

I did not hesitate. I ran wildly from the courtyard and was under the second trapdoor in seconds; I had no ladder, but by clawing and holding on to the wall, I pushed and burst open the trapdoor. I called my wife's name, Henia, quietly at first, then more loudly. The occupants shuffled towards the open trap. They, of course, did not know that the Germans were standing in the next section waiting for a ladder, and they plied me with questions. I grabbed them one by one. There was no time for explanation. "All of you, hide wherever you can," was all I said. They scuttled away.

I walked slowly downstairs and met a German on his way up. "*Jude*, what are you doing here?" he shouted at me. Covered with plaster-dust from the wall, I showed him the number pinned on my jacket and said I had been thirsty and had just come in for a drink. I was now going back to join the workers in the courtyard. He let me go; later, I saw the same officer coming out, quite alone. The inmates had managed to hide successfully and I had miraculously helped to save them. But that was not the end of it.

The Germans left the house with some victims but in the evening before Kol Nidre we got a new order. The Jewish directors of the factory were to search all the flats during the night and send the "illegal" tenants to the station for deportation in the morning. When I heard this, I smuggled my wife out and took her to stay the night with friends who lived outside the block. Meanwhile, the directors prepared themselves for the most tragic of duties. They were being forced to round up fellow-Jews to be murdered—on the Day of Atonement! Fifty workers were selected to carry out the search. I was one of them. Of course, we all decided to search and find no one. The directors, however, took the whole thing seriously and felt that if the "illegals" were sent away, the rest of us would be safe. At ten o'clock at night we, the workers, started on our rounds and told people to hide with as much ingenuity as possible. They were doing this anyway.

One scene I cannot forget. In one room we came upon an old man sitting at a table with a small lamp. He had an open prayer book in front of him and the sound of his melancholy chanting affected us deeply. We begged him to hide. He pointed to a bed in which his wife lay, and we entreated both of them to find somewhere to go. They left the room together somehow, for some secret place.

We came down and reported that we had found no one. One of the directors, a Jew from Vienna, flew into a rage. Such is the instinct of self-preservation. He shouted, "That is impossible! I know there is someone up there." He ran up to the old couple's room, surveyed the disordered bed and touched it, and ran down shouting, "The bed is still warm. Someone must have just left it." We assured him that the room had been empty when we got there. There was nothing else he could do. There were no victims for deportation as a result of our search, but in the morning a few volunteers came forward. I saw a Jewish policeman taking them to the station on Yom Kippur morning. They were all young people; why, I wonder now, did they make this strange decision? Did they hope to save the rest of us or were they just tired of living?

That morning we went to work as we always did. After two hours in the factory, without a word being spoken, we congregated in the main storeroom. Everyone seemed to drift together instinctively. Posting a guard to keep a lookout for SS-man Hoffman or some other German, we started our traditional service. A young man, a tailor, acted as a cantor. He sang sweetly and reduced us all to tears. We returned to work within two hours.

I was restless and apprehensive all day. What had happened to my wife? I could not contact her and could only hope that in her street the night had passed without incident. As soon as the day's work was finished I made my way there, and was overjoyed to find her and our friends safe.

19. The First Ghetto Uprising— January 18th, 1943

ON THE EVENING of January 17th I returned with a group of workers from the Aryan side to the Warsaw ghetto. I had just spent several days outside. We marched to Zamenhof Street and then separated, each of us making his way to a prearranged meeting place. There was a pervading air of restlessness. Dragging wearily through the snow and the pitch darkness, we heard whispers of things to come; rumour had it that people were again to be deported after a few days' respite.

At Mila Street, the first question put to me was, "Why have you come back? Haven't you heard the news?" They could not know that when one lived secretly outside the ghetto it was impossible to hear the faintest whisper about events inside it. And on top of this, the landlady in whose house my wife and I had stayed for some time had felt unhappy and insecure about keeping a male Jewish lodger for longer than was necessary.

I left my small parcel of belongings and hurried to 44, Muranowska Street, hoping to obtain more accurate information. Here in this block lived the officials of the Judenrat who were generally well-informed about German plans of action. While I was there, I went into a relative's flat where a few families lived together. They assured me that in the Judenrat they knew nothing about the projected deportations. I was pressed to stay overnight, but I decided to go back to 61, Mila Street, to other friends who awaited me.

Before leaving, however, I went to see David Goldstein, a former army chaplain, in the same block. In answer to my question about the state of things in the ghetto, he opened a drawer, revealing a loaded revolver. "If they come again, they will pay for it. They will not get me or my child alive." I never saw him again.

It was already after curfew and I rushed anxiously to Mila Street, though, in the main, German patrols avoided the ghetto after nightfall. It was frosty and we huddled round the caretaker's stove at number 64. I was in the company of Yitzhak Giterman, a well-known social worker, a Hebrew scholar called Levene, and a man named Rabinowicz, who had managed to escape from Treblinka. There were also various young resistance workers. Our chief spokesman was Levene, a relative of Chief Rabbi Abraham Kook. His wife and only child had already been deported and he dreamed perpetually of revenge. He said that though very little was possible now, we must go on remembering, and prepare to avenge the crimes committed against us in the not too distant future; we must never forget. Giterman said sadly, "We are preparing to fight, although we know that all is lost." He got up with the others and went to his own home on the opposite side of the street. I left for number 61.

We slept five to a room, warmly covered with a sea of bedclothes left behind by the deportees. One of the five was a Jewish policeman who left to go to his place of work at six in the morning. Half an hour later he was back shouting, "Save yourselves; they are already in the street. Two SS-men have been shot in the courtyard of this house." In seconds we had crawled into the attic through an aperture in the wainscot, and lay flattened between the cavity walls. Until six that night over a hundred people, men, women and children, lay there lethargically, awaiting the worst that could happen. We heard the firing increase in volume and distinguished the sound of marching feet. Suddenly the Germans were in the attic searching and not finding anybody. A deadly silence reigned within the cavity walls. We heard the officers direct commands at the Jewish police. They were to hack down the beams, as our presence was more than suspected. The SS-men went downstairs, saying they would return shortly, and the Jewish policemen did as they were told and chopped away the woodwork. They knew, of course, that we were hidden there, and even who we were. They quickly gave us the latest news. We were told that one resistance worker, a Miss Landau, had been shot while throwing grenades at some Germans who were leading a group of Jews to their execution. She had managed, nevertheless, to aid the escape of a few hundred. We also heard that Yitzhak Giterman had been shot in the street and that a running fight was going on between some Germans and one man who had escaped on to the roof of our house. We lay silently, waiting for a miracle.

The Germans returned. They inspected; they pried; they did not find us. The day dragged by slowly with cold and hunger. When darkness fell, the Germans withdrew, afraid of a new attack from the Jews. We crept out slowly one by one to find, unfortunately, that some of our number were dead, having succumbed to the shock and the horror of the enforced hideaway. Our rooms were completely empty, the furniture and linen gone. We were certain that this was not the end of the crisis. To attempt to use the attic hideaway again was perilous, so we racked our brains to think of another place. As we did so, we were overcome with admiration for the heroism of the Jewish fighters, whose resistance had saved many thousands from certain death.

I went to 64, Mila Street, and saw Yitzhak Giterman's son there. He had been one of my students and he thought his father had been wounded and taken to hospital. I could not bring myself to tell him the truth—that his father had already been buried in a common grave with others who had fallen on the same day.

Among the deported were the officials of the Judenrat with whom I had spoken only the night before. They had been rounded up and sent to Treblinka. I felt completely bewildered, and was hardly able to concentrate when someone told me that the bakery of the same house would make a good hiding place. Friends intervened for me, and so I found myself hidden there with several others for the next seven days. Those days in the bakery were horrific. It was like being entombed, and even now, when I think of it, it still has a nightmarish quality. It was said to be a secure bunker, with hiding space for thirty people; in actual fact, a hundred people crowded in. The entrance was a long narrow tunnel opening alongside the oven door. When everyone was inside, a mountain of coal was heaped up to hide the tunnel mouth, so that no one could suspect that there was anyone there. One had to be very agile to get into the tunnel, and then one had to continue along it on one's stomach, using hands and knees for propulsion. It took at least ten minutes of strenuous pushing to get into the actual bunker at the end. The bunker was made up of two tiny rooms, better described as cupboards. They were so airless that one could not even light a cigarette. The overcrowded conditions can be imagined. Sitting or lying down was out of the question. People were pressed together, supporting each other, all standing.

There was one small electric lamp installed by the owners of the bakery, who had their own families among the crowd. Their children were the only youngsters in the bunker. Though the place seemed safe enough, the danger of discovery was considerable. The SS-men directing operations in the street would stop in the bakery above us, since the bakers had to provide them with food and drinks every day. The slightest noise would have betrayed us. We were terrified because of the children. Everything was done to pacify and soothe them while they stood as wearily and silently as the adults. We had had the unusual good fortune of finding among the belongings, hurriedly thrown together, of the baker's family, a Hagada* published by Schocken in Berlin. This book was lavishly illustrated, and we used the pictures to amuse

* The prayer-book used in the Seder night service on the eve of the Jewish festival of Passover.

and quieten the children while the Germans were eating above us.

The seven days seemed interminable. The younger people, including myself, went out several times in that week, late at night, to get a breath of fresh air; the very old and the very young had to stay put. The effort of dragging in and out of the tunnel would have been too great for them.

At the end of that period, the deportations came to an end.

20. A Night in Hospital

THE MINOR UPRISING of January 1943 was over, with its wealth of drama and heroism. There had been some victorious moments for the Jews, but many victims too. Now "life" in the ghetto began again. Teams of Jewish workers again left to work on the Aryan side, and I decided to join a group in order to try to escape from the ghetto and to contact my wife who had been "outside" for several weeks. At the beginning of November, 1942, we had succeeded in making contact with Polish friends on the other side, to arrange a refuge for her. She left one morning, with a group of women workers, for the "Aryan" side, and did not return.

We departed one frosty morning and the day was filled with hard work at Praga railway station. Our task was to unload coal trucks. The guards seemed to have one main aim—to shorten our lives. There was not a second's break allowed, nor was there any food or water for us. For nine hours they stood over us, using their truncheons as they saw fit. What sustained me was the thought that in the evening I was going to break away from the group on the return journey to the ghetto and go to 12, Franciscan Street, where my wife was hiding. I had arranged this with the Jewish group leader at some cost.

On the way back, I stole away from the group and made my way to Franciscan Street on the Aryan side. This street was only five minutes away from the ghetto walls and was always heavily patrolled by Germans. It was now after six and dark, and curfew was at seven. If I were to find the house gate of number twelve locked, I would be finished. A Jew with no papers wandering on the Aryan side—and I could not even return to the ghetto if I tried! But the gate was open and I went up to the flat where my wife was hidden, knocked twice very gently, and went in as soon as she opened the door. She had not even asked who it was.

During my last week of hiding in the ghetto my wife had been constantly worrying about me—more, even than I did about her. Her landlady, Mrs. Kurowska, tried to convince her that I must be dead and strongly advised her to put all thought of my survival out of her head. Mrs. Kurowska was a simple religious woman and she urged my wife to go to church and have masses said for my soul. Henrietta, however, remained convinced that I was alive. The landlady lived alone in the sizeable flat which she had got after the Jews had been forced into the ghetto, so there was enough space for my wife. Every week Kurowska went off into the country for two or three days, collected a supply of dairy produce, and brought it back to Warsaw where she sold it. This was her livelihood. When she left she always put a padlock on the door, lest snooping neighbours be tempted to investigate. If they had found that she was harbouring a Jew, both she and Henia would have been shot. This state of affairs had been going on for some time. The night before I arrived my wife dreamed that she saw me coming to the house; she told Mrs. Kurowska and begged her not to padlock the door, just this once. Kurowska, superstitious as well as religious, listened and finally gave in. During her absence, my wife, who normally never left the flat, went out and bought some vegetables to make my favourite soup. She cooked it and sat and waited. When she heard my two taps on the door she opened it soundlessly and without alarm. I was speechless with fatigue, hunger and thirst. She merely said, "Sit down and have some soup and I'll tell you about my dream."

I stayed with my wife for three weeks. From the very first day I knew that I could not remain there indefinitely. Apart from being afraid of moving freely in the flat lest the neighbours above and below should hear, and remaining in the dark when Mrs. Kurowska was away as a light would have betrayed our presence, there was also the drawback that Mrs. Kurowska herself was afraid to harbour a man. She would gladly have kept my wife, as she felt it was her patriotic duty to hide someone from the Germans. I had to think fast. Each day seemed like a year. We could not sleep for worry since I had nowhere to go.

There were, however, some happy moments. These were during the days of Stalingrad when the illegal underground press and even the German papers kept us informed of the military communiqués from the front line. We could feel that there had been a reversal in German fortunes. This news was a source of great joy and consolation to us.

Then I remembered a colleague of mine, a former teacher of literature, Jerzy Kreczmar, with whom I had taught for a number of years at a grammar school in Warsaw. I knew he lived in Zoliborz, not far from us, and I decided to visit him by bus. Perhaps he would help me. One Sunday afternoon I slipped out, caught a tram and got to his flat. I knew him to be a broad-minded man, not antisemitic, and I was certain that he would do all he possibly could. I rang the bell and he opened the door himself. I went in and told him my whole story. He was sympathetic but could do nothing. Sitting there, I realised he had a problem of his own: his wife was Jewish. He did not mention her but gave other reasons for his inability to help. Of course I saw his dilemma all to clearly. I departed sadly.

I boarded a tram to return home. To my surprise it stopped en route and went no further. For many reasons, I was anxious to get back, and curfew time was drawing near. People were talking freely and I heard that Franciscan Street had been cordoned off as a German had been shot in the public house at number twelve, in the front of our block. So now I could not even return to my insecure shelter! Looking out of the tram, I saw Germans everywhere. I got off and stood there helpless, lost and without any personal identity papers. It was snowing hard and the cold was bitter. Where could I go? And what had happened to my wife at number twelve?

I had to make some sort of decision quickly. The street was emptying fast and the main gates were being locked for curfew. I found myself in Bonifraterska Street and thought of the famous mental hospital there. Perhaps they would shelter me overnight. I walked there speedily and rang. An elderly, warmly-clad porter opened the door. He pointed to the waiting room, saying, "There are many more in there who could not get home before curfew. You can all spend the night here."

This was a good beginning, at any rate. A warm, brightly-lit room; people sitting and chatting about what had happened during the day; but always the conversation reverted to number 12 Franciscan Street and the German who had been shot there. Everyone was agitated and worrying about his family. I compared my lot with that of the others and felt completely out of place. Above all, I feared that my wife had been taken away by the Germans.

Two nuns entered, said a short prayer and distributed bread and hot coffee to all of us in the waiting room. I controlled my fears as best I could and talked to the others as if I were one of them. Hours passed. At midnight a male nurse came in. He added a few details to what we already knew about the events at number 12 and all the time he talked he stared hard at us. "German policemen often come here at night to get warm," he said. "But don't worry, they will only want to look at your papers." He looked straight at me and continued, "You look like a Jew but don't worry, just show them your papers." I said quietly, "My papers are quite satisfactory. I am not afraid of having them checked." He left the room and I was overcome with terror. I was sure that he would be my executioner. The porter then came in and said that two of us could go into the doctor's office. There were two sofas there and we could stretch out and have a sleep. He pointed to two people, me and another man. Sleep was out of the question—I lay in terror, waiting for the Germans to arrive.

They did not arrive during the night. At six in the morning, I saw the first trams out in the street. Early workers were scurrying along. I prepared to sneak out of the hospital. At the gate I pressed some money into the porter's hand. He had, after all, sheltered me for the night. He would take nothing and said, "I heard what that damned male nurse said to you last night. If the Germans had come, it would have been because he had called them." He added that before the war his daughters had been students at Warsaw University and they were now helping many friends. He did not mention the word Jew. He gave me his name—it was Mendrzycki—and said that he would give me shelter for a night or two when I needed it, in his own flat, which was within the hospital grounds. I knew that he had realised that I was a Jew though he said nothing; I thanked him for his kindness, but never at any time took advantage of his offer. I was frankly afraid of the male nurse and in general the hospital did not feel safe somehow. This porter's act of decency, however, was a long-remembered bright spot in a world of brutality.

I almost ran to 12, Franciscan Street and knocked at the door. A miracle had happened. All the men had been taken away by the Germans but the women were still there. Our landlady saw the hand of God in all this. The fact that I had not spent the night there was, she said, divine intervention. The last few days in the flat were easier for me since she now believed that St. Anthony was personally guarding all three of us.

21. Miracles in Czerniakow

THE DISTRICT OF CZERNIAKOW has always been very well-known in Warsaw. It used to be the centre of the underworld, where all manner of criminal activity took place, from thieving to knifing. The streets were filled with unsavoury characters and before the war no Jew was safe if he walked there after dark. Fate decreed that my wife and I should hide there for two months, in the winter of 1943. Our stay at 12, Franciscan Street had come to an end after three weeks. The landlady began to worry about my presence again and eventually wanted both of us to leave. A friend of ours took great pains to get us "Aryan" papers, and so, when we left number 12, we were no longer Jews. My wife was Antonina Jozwiak, a Catholic of course, and I was Jan Zielinski, also Catholic. These papers gave us security of a sort, but we knew full well that though they had photographs and the swastika stamp, they would never pass scrutiny at Gestapo headquarters. They could delude us into a certain sense of security, but no one else. We left number 12 just before curfew, and went to Czerniakow by a "droshky", a long and dangerous route.

We had been recommended to a religious Catholic family. They were very poor but kind and anxious to help. The members of the family were an eighty-year-old grandmother, her daughter Klima in her fifties, and a grandson, aged about twenty-five. Their home, one room and a kitchen, was in a small house in the middle of a common, not far from the main street in the district. The rear of the house was occupied by a woman and her two daughters who often held wild parties. They entertained very dubious people, including uniformed Germans.

Our poor family were keen to have us without rent at a time when people were taking enormous sums to hide Jews. They had no previous knowledge of us but felt they had a sacred duty to shelter anyone in need. Of course, our existence had to be a closely-guarded secret. During the daytime we crept on all fours so that no one should see us through the window of the little home. During the two months we were there, my wife and I scarcely spoke to each other, so that strange voices might not be overheard by the neighbours. Mrs. Klima had to buy food for us in a different shop from the one she normally used. Her own grocer and milkman would have guessed that she was buying for more than the usual three people. Both the grandmother and her daughter prayed frequently that God would help them and us. When we were worried that something might happen, they always assured us that they would stand by us and protect us. Their compassion was outstanding.

Easter was getting closer and a new problem arose for us. Mrs. Klima said she had to go to confession and that she had to tell the whole truth. That included telling about us. She was afraid that the priest might not approve and regard this procedure as dangerous; she was at a loss what to do, and asked me for advice. I begged her let us know what day she was going to confession, so that we could stay out of the house all day. Thus she would not need to mention us and would have a clear conscience. We kept out of the house that day, as promised, but Mrs. Klima confessed everything to the priest! Happily for us and for her, however, the priest assured her that she was performing a noble service in helping those in danger. She returned home overjoyed. Yet circumstances were so hard, and got so much harder as the days lengthened, that we decided that I would leave and my wife would stay. I went to Skolimow near Warsaw to work with friends, taking a job as a gardener. Nevertheless, my wife's stay was also short-lived, for the following reason. One day, when only the grandmother and my wife were in the house, sitting as quiet as mice, Henrietta heard a conversation through the wall. The neighbour, Mrs. Kaminska, and a relative of hers were talking. Mrs. Kaminska said she had a feeling that a Jewess was hiding next door. The relative said she should inform the Germans at once, and they would soon find out if it were true. When my wife heard this she ran out of the house in terror and never went back. The grandmother, old and deaf, had not heard the conversation and, seeing Henrietta jump up, signalled to her not to go outside. Henrietta quietened her by whispering in her ear that she would soon return. This was their only farewell. The next day the house was searched and nothing found.

All this is really an introduction to the miracle I experienced during the time that I was in the house in Czerniakow Common. When we first hid there together I left the house a few times, risking my life to buy a few necessities in the nearby shops. I used to go in the early evening, when it was dark in winter, and when there were few people around because of the bad weather.

One day, coming out of a shop in the main street, I saw a familiar face. It belonged to a cousin of mine, Naomi Zylberberg, who had also managed to escape from the ghetto. She was the only one of the immediate family who had got out and she was now living near us in Czerniakow. We were both overjoyed. She was more satisfactorily situated than we were, but visiting her was out of the question and she could not, of course, come to us. She told me she had a Jewish friend near her who spent his time faking documents for many Jews who required them. I told her I was worried about our documents as they were so badly made and asked if she could help. We arranged a time and place to meet the man and discuss my proposition with him.

A few days later I went as arranged to the tram terminal at Wilanow. He was waiting for me, and even at a distance I recognised him from my cousin's description. As I moved towards him I sensed the presence of two Polish policemen closing in on me. I could not turn round now. The policemen, with a crowd of young street lads following, came up and asked both of us for our papers. The document-maker was immediately bewildered, although I knew him to have a sound set of personal documents in the name of Borkowski. He pulled a packet of fakes out of his pocket and, turning, threw them into a clump of bushes. The lads rushed to collect them for the police and both of us were marched to the police station. I had nothing to say. It was obvious to the police that they had caught two Jews. The danger of our position was increased since German patrols often passed that way, and if they had seen us being arrested our lives would have been ended on the spot. Our way led towards the common where I lived in hiding with my wife. I made one desperate move. I asked the police if we could buy our freedom. It was an open bribe which they would not accept. They felt that the Jews should be repaid for co-operating with the Russians in eastern Poland when the Bolsheviks occupied that territory. The younger policeman of the two was particularly firm on this point since he said he had been to Lwow and noticed Jews fraternising openly with Russians. My companion listened, downcast and resigned. He did not even try to reason with the police. We were practically at the station—and once inside our fate was sealed.

I tried to talk to the police and said that we could not be held responsible for what had happened in other towns. I told them that I myself was born in Plock, had studied and worked till the war in Warsaw, and had stayed there right until now. As soon as I mentioned the word "Plock", the younger policeman stopped in his tracks. "That's my home town too," he said, "I know all the Jews of Plock." It transpired that we were brought up in the same street and he did, indeed, know my family. All pretence ceased from that instant and I told him my real name. The atmosphere had changed. We stopped on the pavement and I asked with renewed heart, "How much?" They were prepared to release us both for 5,000 zlotys.

I did not possess anything like that amount of money but my companion said he would bring it to them. The policemen agreed, but said they would keep me as a hostage until he came back. This was very risky for me. I was not certain that the other would return. Life was very cheap at that time and my unknown companion might have been only too glad to escape. In addition, the policemen might very well pocket the money and then turn us over to the Germans. This had often been known to happen. But I just had to agree; there was no alternative. I counted the slowly-passing minutes and eventually "Borkowski" was seen hurrying back, with the money. We were both released. I returned home after dark and long after curfew. Mrs. Klima and my wife had been very worried about me, but I did not tell them anything. I did not see Naomi or Mr. Borkowski again.

After the war I found my cousin, who had been freed from Bergen-Belsen. She now lives in Melbourne, Australia, with her family.

22. Gardening in Skolimow

IT IS APRIL, 1943. I have now been at Skolimow near Warsaw for five weeks. Polish friends of pre-war days have agreed to let me work as their gardener. They feel that I could easily pass as an Aryan. I do not look particularly "Jewish"; in fact I am rather typically Polish. I speak Polish like a native and, above all, they really do need someone to do the garden and prepare it for the spring planting. I found it hard to decide about taking this open-air job as a Catholic and as a professional gardener. Most worrying of all was the thought that I would be constantly visible to all who passed the house and its grounds. But I accepted the job and set to work. The five weeks passed quickly and the perpetual hard work became a source of pleasure to me.

The nuns who pass by wonder why I work so hard and give me the customary Catholic greeting to which I make response.

A few more Jews were shot in the township today. They belonged to a group of Jewish intellectuals who had tried to find a hiding place in this elegant resort.

Now I am back in my room, thinking and writing about the past. I remember the two lodgers with whom my wife and I shared a flat in the days before the destruction of the Warsaw ghetto. They lived with us for about a year and shared with us the miseries of those days. They were our constant companions until they died.

One of these lodgers was a lady called Johanna Lamm, née Heine. Until 1938 she had lived with her husband in Stettin and was, like other members of her family, completely assimilated. Many years previously she had married a Jew of Polish extraction and was therefore expelled with him from Germany to Zbonszyn, a town on the frontier of Poland and Germany. She remained proud of her German nationality, of her German culture; but above all, of her family's patriotism. She had three brothers, two of whom had fallen *für das Vaterland* during the First World War. The third had continued working as sanitary engineer in the Public Health Department of Hamburg during the Nazi régime. He was affectionately known as *der Wasser Heine*. Johanna herself had volunteered for service in a military hospital in 1914 and displayed the certificates and prizes she had won at Stettin. From Zbonszyn she and her husband came to Warsaw, but early in the war he was arrested by the Germans when they found a radio set in the block in which they lived. She always hoped that her husband would return, but in the meantime found comfort in the companionship of another woman whose marriage had been disrupted in the same way.

In 1941 Janusz Korczak suggested that these two women move in with us into our one-room flat, making the kitchen their bedroom. So our life together as one family began. It was then that they told us about their earlier lives and their families. They were both over fifty, lonely and absolutely assimilated; the one completely German, the other completely Polish.

In that desperate summer of 1942 I had to think for all of us. The danger increased day by day and one could think of nothing but staying alive. There was no doubt in my mind that a suitable hiding place would have to be found. One night I and a few friends prepared a shelter in a cellar below the block of flats where we now lived, at 17, Chlodna Street. We bricked in the main entrance and improvised a trapdoor in the floor of a shop as the entrance. We could hide a hundred people there. When things became really hazardous, the tenants would go down at six o'clock in the morning and spend most of the day in hiding. Mrs. Heine-Lamm would not come down with us since it was impossible to convince her that she, too, was in danger. She had collected her certificates gained as a military nurse in the First World War, her family papers, and data relating to her two brothers who had fallen on active service. The particulars of her brothers' deaths were inscribed in a prayer book which she had brought with her from Stettin to Warsaw. She was certain that she would be left in peace and not join those taken to the "East".

Another factor that contributed to her lack of concern for her personal safety was that there were many Germans, some Nazis even, in her family. She had often received letters and parcels from her brother-in-law, Dr. Brandt of Breslau, and from her nephew, an SS officer. She, being childless, had brought up the nephew and they were devoted to each other. Mrs. Heine-Lamm even boasted of receiving letters from Field Marshal von Mackensen who was an old friend of her family. All this mail had come to her while she lived in our flat in the ghetto and I myself had read some of it, in which enquiries were made about her present conditions. Clutching all these documents she kept saying, "After all, I am German. . . ."

One day in August, 1942, some SS officers surrounded the block which included 17, Chlodna Street. Nearly all the tenants were hidden in the cellar and a friend and I mounted guard. We sensed imminent danger and we had warned one of the tenants, the famous painter Roman Kramsztyk, to come down with us.

He seemed quite oblivious and stood calmly smoking his pipe. We slipped into the cellar in time to hear the shouts of SS officers calling repeatedly for the caretaker, but he, also, was hidden with his family. They searched the block for over two hours and we, panic-stricken, heard them stamping on the shop floor above our heads; from time to time, a shot was fired, and we knew that someone had been caught. Long afterwards, when we felt it safe to come out, we found that a number of people had been killed. They lay in the courtyard, on the stairs, even in their beds. The painter was dead and Johanna Heine-Lamm was lying with her papers in a pool of blood.

The sad tale is mainly for you, Dr. Brandt, and for your son, the SS officer, who was always so anxious for news of his dear aunt. If you went on writing, this is why your letters were returned marked "Unknown". . . .

Added in London

I have now checked with the volume *Ein Gedenkbuch*, published in Berlin, 1933, and found the names of the two brothers, Fritz and Hans Heine of Stettin, who fell fighting for Germany in 1915.

23. The Ghetto Uprising, April 1943

I WAS NOW an old Skolimow inhabitant and an experienced gardener. At first I was afraid to go out and about freely; now I moved around the estate with ease. I felt a little safer, since obviously no one suspected that I was a Jew. In spite of this, I was sad and plagued by misfortune, dreaming constantly of those who were gone; acutely aware of my odd position in this society, I was always lonely and invariably on the alert. These tensions made life almost unbearable. It is hard to believe that, in this beautiful environment, I should have yearned to be back in the ghetto. I wanted to be back with those few who were still alive in Warsaw. I longed to be among them, to share their fate.

One must admit, also, that a Jew who was caught on the Aryan side fared worse, perhaps, than the Jew in the ghetto. Death itself was not so bad, but the prolonged torture, mockery and humiliation which preceded it were ten times worse. When it happened to an isolated and betrayed Jew, he was completely demoralised. The crowds in the ghetto could derive some shred of comfort in facing death together; alone, one was the single focus of all hostile, depraved, insulting and manic words and actions.

The Passover festival was drawing closer and this, also, made me want to return to the ghetto. I got a few days' leave of absence, joined a group of Polish workers who went there every day and, with them, marched back in on April 13th, 1943. I was determined to stay inside over the festival. As soon as we arrived, I left the workers and soon saw many familiar faces, including some of my relations. As I approached Zamenhof Street I was quickly surrounded by a group of people who eagerly asked me how things were on the "other side". I stared at them, hardly recognising some of them. How they had changed in two or three months! Bodies bent double with care and hunger; lacklustre eyes; and complete resignation on all faces. I met people who, a short while ago, had been active community workers, earning a decent living, men of acute intelligence; now they were as careworn, thin and hopeless as the rest. Some of them had formed contacts with the Aryan side but for various reasons had not left the ghetto. Many of them begged me to find hiding places for them "outside" or at least for a child who had somehow stayed alive; a few offered large sums of money. They would have given all they had to save one person dear to them, but they remained indifferent to their own fate.

When I told them that I was determined to stay in the ghetto during Passover they looked at me first with amazement, then with sympathy. They, so anxious to be out—I, so desperate to be in, if only for a short while! The gulf that separated these two sets of emotions and the circumstances that fostered them almost defy comprehension.

I walked from Zamenhof Street to Mila Street to see the people with whom I had stayed before leaving. I met many friends, among them the outstanding group who were organising the uprising and who were now in command of the ghetto. There was open discussion of resistance in the event of a new German round-up and mass deportations. Everyone was preparing to celebrate the Passover, but felt that I was mad to stay at such a time, since the Germans made a point of choosing Jewish festivals for their surprise attacks. I stayed, however, for three days and left on the seventeenth, in the evening, with the Polish workers' group. That period showed me very clearly how real the danger was and people begged me so repeatedly to leave that my stay, fortunately as it turned out, was shorter than intended. Though I call the band with whom I left and entered a "workers' group", this designation is inaccurate. They had bribed the Germans to give them work permits to enable them to enter the ghetto; once inside, they bought valuable articles from Jews who sold readily and cheaply. It was essentially a business arrangement; people were selling all their household goods and linen for which they had no further use.

As soon as we got out of the ghetto I left the group and went to visit my wife who was in hiding nearby, then hurried back to Skolimow. My wife knew about my intended visit and was anxious to see me again and to hear how things were for those still inside. Two days later I was hard at work again in the garden, and had no idea what was happening in the ghetto. In the evening, my employer, Czeslaw Piotrkowicz, returned from Warsaw where he worked during the day, and brought the tragic news that the Germans had again started massive deportations—but the Jews were resisting. I shuddered, knowing that this fight meant the end of the ghetto and everyone in it. Total victory for the Jews inside was out of the question.

That evening, the nineteenth, was the eve of Passover, and I prepared to commemorate the festival in my own small way as best I could. I went out into the forest and heard the reverberation of the distant gunfire. Sleep was impossible; this was to be a night of wakefulness—a *Lail Shimurim*;* I was to hold my own vigil and service, alone, living through their experience on this night of "blood, fire and pillars of smoke". These words, from the Hagada, had acquired a new meaning.

* A watchful night; the first night of Passover. See Exodus XII: 42.

In the morning, I resolved to go into town. Perhaps someone would be able to give me up-to-date information about the Uprising. Perhaps I would be able to do something. What, I did not know. In the train, everybody was talking about the ghetto fight and saying that it could not last long. But life and activity in the town were as normal as ever, as if nothing at all had occurred in that one section of it. I went to my employer's flat in Marszalkowska Street. Piotrkowicz and his relatives were shattered at what had happened; they knew that this was the end of Warsaw Jewry. He told me that friends of mine in the ghetto had just telephoned him; they had managed to escape, and were speaking to him from town, begging him to ask me to help. I waited for them —but neither saw nor heard from them again.

Later in the day I wandered over to Miodowa Street, nearer and nearer to the ghetto. Thousands of people were walking towards it, to go and look at the strange spectacle. On Plac Krasinskich, near the ghetto wall, the Germans had organised a fair. Tuneful, light melodies filled the air and the crowd was enjoying the bright lights and music as if this, indeed, were all. The detonations from the Jewish quarter mingled with the music coming over the loudspeakers in the fair.

I went back to my friend and employer in Marszalkowska Street and asked him if I could stay the night. I could be contacted there if my help was required. He agreed.

It was dusk, and the sky was deep red on the horizon. Smoke from the ghetto hung like a pall over half the town. The windows of the house, some distance from the fighting, rattled with every burst of gunfire. All night I thought of those falling and dying in the combat against the cruellest of our enemies and compared them with myself and other fugitives like me—so lacking in true heroism. Thoughts crowded in on me all night; I felt that from their blood a new life, full of hope, would spring—like a phoenix from the ashes. As the prophet Ezekiel had said, *"Bedamaich Chaii"*— "By your blood, you shall live!" But the thoughts of many people around me in Marszalkowska Street were vastly different. They thought the noise was part of the traditional Catholic firework display and gunfire salute that marked the Feast of the Resurrec-

The badge on this German officer's belt proclaims: "God is with us"

The ruins of the Tlomackie Synagogue, destroyed by the SS (see page 118)

 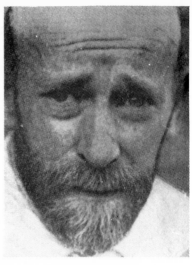

Rabbi Judah Zlotnik-Avrida—the photograph found by the author in the ghetto ruins (see page 170)

Dr. Janusz Korczak

Dr. Korczak's letter to the author (see page 44) bearing the heading of the ghetto orphanage

„POMOC DLA SIEROT"
w WARSZAWIE

Warszawa, dn. 29 sierpnia .... 194 1 r.

DOM SIEROT
Krochmalna 92
obecnie Chlodna 33

Wielmożny Pan

Zylberberg

W miejscu

Szanowny Panie.

Z wielu racyj pragniemy, by nabożeństwa świąteczne odbyły się w Domu Sierot, - z różnych źródeł płyną też i obawy, żeby to, co powinno być poważne i czyste, nie wyszło niemądrze i mętnie.

Jeżeli Pan X nie będzie mógł zdobyć mizernej sumy na poczet wydatków, jakże ufać, że uda mu się zmontować należycie rzecz wcale niełatwą?

Stanowisko wygodne dla Zarządu: niech Dyrekcja sama decyduje, - nakłada tem większy obowiązek ostrożności i odpowiadzialności za decyzję.

Z szacunkiem

Dyrektor Domu Sierot i Bursy

tion. Coming as it did from the ghetto, it was divine symbolism . . .
yet not all Poles felt this way. There were many Poles who were
sorrowful at the destruction of the ghetto. But they, also, had to
conceal their feelings from the others, who openly demonstrated
their indifference.

Now, I longed to leave Warsaw; I wanted to be as far as possible
from the tumult. An order had been issued by Dr. Fischer, the
governor of the city, to the effect that any hidden Jew must
be handed over to the Germans. Failure to comply carried the
death penalty, and posters proclaiming this were displayed on
all street corners. I made my way to Wilanow Station and queued
for a ticket to Skolimow. In front of me was a crowd of men and
women, chatting and laughing, discussing the fighting in the
ghetto. I kept looking at the red and smoky sky. Suddenly I heard
somebody from the queue asking the booking clerk for a ticket
"*Do Cadyka*"—"to the Rabbi". Another man did the same. For a
second I was stupefied, then I realised they meant a ticket to the
town of Ger (Gora Kalvaria), which, before the war, had been
the home of a very famous Chassidic Rabbi. The clerk showed
no surprise at their request; he understood it well.

In the train, I sat in the same carriage as a group of men whom,
from their conversation, I judged to be on the editorial board of
the Polish Nazi paper, *Nowy Kurier Warszawski*. They all lived at
Skolimow. They were in good spirits and talked endlessly about
the resistance in the ghetto, being of the opinion that in twenty-
four hours it would all be over and that Warsaw would be rid of
its Jews, who had poisoned the atmosphere for far too long.
Worn out, I arrived in Skolimow. I prepared for my day's work
in the garden as if nothing had happened.

For days and nights the echoes of the fighting in the Warsaw
ghetto have been quite audible to us here, although this place is
about 20 kilometres from the city. The nights are particularly
terrible. One can see the sky glowing with distant fires. In the deep
silence the bombing is frightening and there one has no desire to
sleep. I usually spend hours in the forest which verges on the garden. The silence is palpable, broken intermittently by the croaking of

frogs and the rustling of trees. The only consolation for me is to repeat to myself the psalms that I still remember. My thoughts turn to the ruined ghetto and I wonder who is still alive, if anyone is alive at all.

24. Sunday in Skolimow

IT IS SUNDAY. From early morning the day has been beautiful and in the garden I can see the results of my hard work. The flowers and the vegetables are growing fast and this gives me a lot of pleasure. As usual, I am free on Sundays, and I can sleep longer. But I must plan how to spend this long day. It is a recurring problem every Sunday, and not easily solved because I am afraid of everyone.

The local people go to church in the morning, leaving the village almost deserted. Even so, I cannot risk mingling with them in their place of worship since they are all known to each other and a stranger in their midst would arouse curiosity. I have thought a lot recently about the attitude of some of these religious churchgoers. It is significant that the churches are always packed with people queuing for Mass and Evensong, and yet one has to be wary of them. On the other hand, I must add that I have come to appreciate the courage and high moral standards of some of these people who have given shelter and sympathised with us because of the crimes committed in recent months by the Germans.

It is already eleven o'clock and I must find something to occupy myself with until lunchtime. As the weather is good I walk down to the stream and try to enjoy the surroundings. Other people are doing the same and they pay no attention to me, unlike the worshippers in the church.

Quite suddenly I feel that something is wrong. An SS van is driving from town towards the village. Everyone is nervous, but no one more so than I. Who knows—it is possible that its destination is my employer's house, that it is coming for *me*. The van turns right and this means that it is going to Chylice, another village in the neighbourhood. I am disturbed and stay where I am, not risking the walk back to our village, Skolimow. In half an hour it is all over. The van with its smiling officers returns; its story preceded it. A Jewish family—an old man, a middle-aged woman and three children—had been hiding in the village. They were all shot and their bodies are now lying outside the house, in the garden. The news is widely discussed here and people wonder how the Germans got information about the Jews in hiding.

I return to lunch heartbroken, obsessed with what has just happened. I must do something to divert my mind from the tragedy. So I remember our second lodger in the ghetto. . . .

Part of the original Yiddish MS. of a "*A Warsaw Diary*" (greatly reduced). It was written at Skolimow and recovered in 1964.

Our second lodger was called Gisella Hernes, née Neufeld, the one who had come with Johanna Heine-Lamm to live with us. Her ancestors had been among the foremost Jewish families in nineteenth-century Poland. Her grandfather, Daniel Neufeld, editor of the Polish-Jewish magazine, *Jutrzenka*, was sent to Siberia for participation in the Polish uprising of 1863. Gisella had been a well-known pianist, and had won awards in many European capitals. She and her husband lived in Berlin after their marriage but later they moved to Torun in Poland, where he flourished as a rich industrialist.

Gisella Hernes, middle-aged and childless, was lonely after her husband's arrest. He had been taken with Mrs. Lamm's husband when the radio set was found in the block in Sosnowa Street. Gisella often came to visit Dr. Janusz Korczak's orphanage when she was in the ghetto and I had met her there before she moved into our flat. She impressed everyone with her charm and ability, and Korczak always spoke of her with admiration.

From 22nd July, 1942, when the extermination programme proper began, Gisella was completely shattered. She sensed the danger even more than the others and often used to say that we should never surrender alive. We tried to calm her but to no avail.

The following Friday, I came home with shocking news. I had learned that Adam Czerniakow, the Chairman of the Judenrat, had just committed suicide in sheer despair. He felt that he could not comply with the German order to authorise the despatch of Jews to the "East". The same day one of our closest relations had been taken away. A Jewish police officer, Schwalbe, to whom I had spoken, felt that the situation was hopeless for all of us. He committed suicide a few days later.

The table was set for the Friday evening meal; my wife lit the candles and invited our two lodgers to supper. I tried to create the normal atmosphere, but could not, as the events of the day had greatly affected me. One could see that Mrs. Hernes-Neufeld was not really with us; she was irritable and could not eat. She excused herself early and went to bed. Soon afterwards we heard what seemed to be a hum of conversation. This was, in fact, Mrs. Hernes praying aloud, asking for mercy for children and the helpless. Then silence filled the room.

After supper Mrs. Heine-Lamm went to visit neighbours and I went to a tenants' meeting in the block. I asked my wife to go and sit with Mrs. Hernes. She was resting peacefully in bed but was very glad to see Henrietta. She talked endlessly about multitudes of Jews sleeping quietly and free from fear; in her mind's eye, she saw them seated around tables decked with Sabbath candles, as in the room she had so recently left. Suddenly she said, "I am so tired," and turned over and fell asleep. My wife told me all this when I came back after the meeting.

Next morning at six o'clock we prepared to go down to our shelter. Mrs. Lamm hurried in, saying that she could not wake her friend Gisella. I tried without success and realised that something was wrong. I called in a neighbouring doctor, who found a half empty bottle of veronal in her room, and said she had to be taken to hospital at once. We might be able to save her life. We took her there in a handcart; but the doctors felt that it might be kinder not to awaken her. She died three days later and I saw her, still smiling, in the hospital mortuary. She was buried in a communal grave, where and when I never found out. I found a letter in her room addressed to my wife. With the letter there was a dose of veronal, sufficient to kill one person. She wrote that she regretted having only the one dose, and that we should cast lots for it. We kept it for a long time, but finally decided to fight together to the end. The tablets were thrown away.

It is now dark outside and I am thinking about today's victims and the sad story of Mrs. Hernes-Neufeld. In recording it, I feel temporarily less isolated. Writing has briefly replaced the need for human contact.

25. Hiding in Chylice

I HAD BEEN WORKING as a gardener at Skolimow for two months. In spite of all the difficulties and hardships which beset me, I felt happy for two reasons. First, working hard from dawn to dusk did not leave me much time to think. Secondly, my employers, pre-war friends, knew that I was a Jew; so I did not need to do any play-acting in their company. I hoped, and went on deceiving myself, that this was the ideal spot for me and that I could stay here indefinitely.

It was a sunny May day, the seventeenth to be exact, 1943. Everything was in blossom. On one side the flower beds were ablaze with colour, on the other, young green vegetables were sprouting. I felt proud of my labours. It was silent and peaceful, with not a soul in sight. I had become quite an expert at my work, and it gave me as much pleasure as my previous more complex existence as student and teacher. Today my task was to plant some tomatoes.

My employer Czeslaw Piotrkowicz appeared on the scene quite suddenly. He had hurried back from Warsaw. Seeing him in the middle of the day made me immediately suspicious since he did not generally come back until evening. He did not make for the house, but coming towards me, called out, "Janie, Janie—John, John! Leave at once! There's danger!" I realised that someone from Skolimow must have warned him, so I said nothing; but in a matter of minutes, having dropped everything, I was on my way to Warsaw. It turned out that neighbours had indeed suspected the presence of a Jew working there and had reported this to the police, and that someone had secretly informed my employer of what was afoot. The next day the police searched the whole house and found nothing.

I wandered around Warsaw for days and felt that it would be better for me to look for another hideout not far from Skolimow than stay in the city. Skolimow itself, of course, was barred to me, so I decided to go to Chylice, a village a little way beyond it. When I arrived there, I traipsed around the little country hamlet, scrutinising the streets and houses, and came upon a house standing secluded on a sandy hillock. I liked the look of the place and felt that it would be safer there than in a house which was one of a closely-built group of structures.

I went into the garden of the secluded house and met an old man. He must have been about eighty and was the owner of the property. Very diplomatically, I got into conversation with him. I told him about my work in Warsaw, about relatives of mine, about friends. I wanted to test his responses. Though I was fighting for my life, I always tried to assume that the people I met tended to be compassionate and not vindictive. It was a guiding principle of mine to refuse to believe that everyone was bloodthirsty; and to see that the old, especially, were treated with a dignity and respect that befitted their years.

I was impressed with this elderly man. He seemed very interested in everything I told him, and so I decided to pursue my real purpose. I asked him if it would be possible to rent a room in his house, just for one month. I would only be sleeping there, when I returned at night from my work in Warsaw. He agreed gladly. He led me to a room on the first floor and asked a ridiculously small amount, fifty zlotys a month. From the amount he asked it was obvious that he had no idea that I was a Jew. The room was very pleasant and had a balcony overlooking the garden. This was an added point in its favour—it was a useful escape route. Another happy feature was that, apart from himself, the other sole occupant of the house was his twin sister. After our negotiations, and after I had paid one month's rent in advance, the old man told me about himself. As soon as he started talking and mentioned his name, I was appalled. He was called Grunwald! Surely he was a German laying a trap for me! He continued his story. He was a locksmith by trade and a widower, but once had two sons. In his own words, "The Huns killed them. Those devils should be totally wiped out." I relaxed and began to trust him, in spite of his name.

Every morning I left for Warsaw and got the last train back before curfew. Both the brother and the sister treated me kindly and I felt comfortable with them. In the evening, they would leave a pint of hot milk for me; I had not asked for it. The brother, to show his welcome, picked a plateful of cherries for me every day. Often, when I returned, all the doors were wide open, as the twins were visiting their neighbours, but the milk and the cherries were always there. The contrast between the clatter and tumult of Warsaw and this pretty secluded corner gave a new meaning to the Hebrew expression, "From slavery to freedom". I gradually ceased worrying completely about their name—Grunwald.

The old man loved alcohol and drank heavily all day. This might have disturbed me, but I accepted his drunkenness as normal, since during the war everyone who could drank a great deal. People were trying to blot out the bitterness of reality.

I had paid the rent but, unhappily, did not see out my four weeks' residence. It started with an episode in the nearby forest. In the evenings, returning from Warsaw, tired of walking the streets, the cemeteries and churches, I used to avoid the main road of Chylice and took a forest path to the house instead. This, I thought, would be safer. On this path one evening I met three of the young layabouts from the village. They blocked my way, and one snatched my bag while the other two grabbed me. They said, "We will soon establish who you are at the police station." I pretended not to understand and asked, "What's the matter? By the way, all I possess is that bag and the loaf in it. It is senseless to attack a poor worker." They held my arms pinned fast behind my back and said they knew where I lived and that deception would not help me. The word *Jude*, the worst term that could be used, was not uttered. Yet it was obvious that they suspected it.

As always, in that sort of situation, a bit of cheek came in useful. Anyhow, I had nothing to lose. It was getting darker and was nearly curfew, when we all had to be off the streets. I had to think fast. I said sharply:

"Of course, it is easy to attack an unarmed man, especially when it's three against one. Aren't you ashamed of yourselves? When I was your age, Poland was also in danger, but then we were all in the army. I, as an officer, fought for our country. Now that country is occupied by an enemy and people are suffering, yet you play games and attack helpless travellers in a forest. It is a crime to do such a thing."

My words stopped them dead in their tracks. I noticed the effect I was having even while I spoke. They let me go, gave me back the bag and warned me to avoid the forest, as the people around were suspicious of me.

I stayed at the house for a few more days. During that time, however, I had a new experience even more disturbing than the episode in the forest.

Returning one evening at dusk when it was raining hard, I reached the house and found it empty. The old people were out visiting. Shortly after I had settled down in my room, I heard strange footsteps mounting the stairs. I had learned to recognise the old couple's tread. The steps were coming towards my room. The door opened and a drunkard stamped in, the owner of a nearby house, and demanded money for alcohol. He said he knew I was a Jew. He added that he had a list of all the Jews hidden in Chylice and they all gave him money, but he did not interfere with them in any other way. I laughed at him and said I had no dealings with drunkards; he was talking nonsense because he was tipsy. Of course, I was prepared to have a drink with a neighbour— but tomorrow, when he was sober. He walked out, but I saw that instead of returning to his own home, he went into the main street. It looked as if he might be going to the police station to inform them of the Jew in hiding. It was still pouring with rain and it was pitch black. Now, however, I knew I could not spend the night in this room. I slipped out and ran into the forest. What now?

I remembered a fellow worker who used to talk to me when I worked in Skolimow. He lived in Chylice and I knew his address. I thought I would try my luck and see if I could get a bed there for the night. When I got to his house, the whole family, husband, wife and child, were in bed. I told them I had missed the train to Warsaw; it was very late, and would it be possible for me to spend the night with them? It was easy to see that they were suspicious of the whole story. The house was a one-roomed wooden structure which contained the bed, some chairs and a table. They both got up and asked me to sit down and wait. I did not know when, or with whom, they might return. I was afraid to stay and ran back to the forest to wait developments; I could watch the house from there. After half an hour they returned with no police escort, so I ran back and they told me that the man's brother had said I could stay overnight but had to leave in the morning. I lay on a sack of straw on the floor, awake and counting the hours, and anxious to get an early train to Warsaw.

At five in the morning I prepared to take my leave. I wanted to thank my hosts for their hospitality, and walked up to the bed, but the husband addressed me first. "You have had a lot of luck. I knew who you were, but my brother and I decided to shelter you for one night. But you must pay for it—one thousand zlotys." It was a bargain at the price. I had the money with me, paid, thanked him profusely and got the first train back to Warsaw. I never went to Chylice again.

This is Warsaw, 1946. I switch on the wireless and hear the news at 7 a.m. I hear, among other local items, that Mr. Grunwald of Chylice has been decorated for his heroism during the war. He, as a locksmith, had produced armaments for the underground and his house had been a refuge for the partisans. When I was in hiding there, the Germans were already keeping an eye on the house and had, in fact, shot both the sons of the old man. My tranquil paradise had been a powder keg.

26. The House in Sapiezynska Street

SAPIEZYNSKA STREET is in Warsaw, near the centre of the old Jewish quarter, and not so far from Nalewki Street and Franciscan Street. Till the outbreak of war the block that was number seven was totally occupied by Jews; only the porter and his family were Catholics. In 1943, it was excluded from the ghetto and so the houses were comparatively undamaged. It was tenanted by a mixture of Catholics from all strata of society.

When my wife left the ghetto at the end of 1942, our friends, the Piotrkowiczes, found an initial hiding place for her with a family who lived at number seven Sapiezynska Street. They knew that my wife was Jewish and had escaped from the Germans, but were willing to take her for a very high monthly payment. The husband, Jan Witkowski, was as poor as a church mouse with not a shirt to his back or a penny to his pocket. This financial transaction suited him very well; he had never in his life seen such a large amount of money.

Their life together, however, did not last very long. After a week Jan Witkowski said he was afraid of risking his life any further. He could not sleep at night for worrying about it. He wanted my wife to leave forthwith, and so she did. I heard all this from her much later; I did not know the Witkowskis and both Henrietta and I forgot the brief episode of her stay with them.

Months passed, and the summer of 1943. Because of my precarious situation at Skolimow, I had always sought to provide myself with an additional address at which I could hide, an escape route in the event of catastrophe. I had many friends, but not many could provide me with a shelter which I could use in an emergency. I suddenly remembered the Witkowskis at Sapiezynska Street. Perhaps they would take me as a lodger. I knew, however, that I would have to present myself as a Catholic worker, looking for work in Warsaw. From what I knew of the family, I thought I might stand a chance of lodging with them. They were simple naïve people and could not imagine that any Jew would pose as a Christian and, above all, would attempt to lodge in their flat so near the ghetto. It was also obvious to everyone that no Jew would want to be in the vicinity so soon after the Uprising. Here the danger was still greater than in any other section of the city.

I nevertheless decided to pursue my original idea, but wanted to get a "reference" from a good family which I could show to them. Mr. Piotrkowicz allowed me to use his name and say I was a friend of his. So, dressed in a worker's garb, I went to see Witkowski. It was a sunny afternoon and he was decorating his flat. I introduced myself as Jan Zielinski, who worked in Warsaw, and asked if it would be possible to lodge with him and his family. I mentioned Piotrkowicz's name, and Witkowski and his wife were wonderfully impressed and declared themselves proud to lodge any friend of the Piotrkowiczes who were a rich Catholic family. Witkowski, in fact, rose in his own esteem; what an honour that such a man should recommend his friend to lodge in this humble dwelling!

He clambered off his ladder and introduced me to his wife and two little daughters of three and six. The whole idea of having a lodger seemed to delight him greatly, and he hurried to show me a bed in a dark alcove. He asked as a rental fifty zlotys a month, a ludicrously small amount, particularly when compared with the thousands of zlotys my wife had had to pay for the same bed. I agreed at once and paid a month's rent in advance. Thus I acquired a roof over my head for a year, right up to the Uprising of General Bor Komorowski in 1944.

During the conversation I had with Mr. Witkowski, he stressed several times that he could not get rid of the fleas and bedbugs left behind by the Jews. He had tried twice to repaint the whole flat, but Jewish grime and dirt clung to everything. I pretended not to understand his complaints against the previous Jewish occupiers. Perhaps I should not have taken the lodgings, but I could not risk Skolimow and Chylice much longer and had no choice but to sink into the bosom of the family. I kept up the rent, and had the place as a base to return to when Skolimow and the next village, Chylice, proved too hot for me. My mobility was in my favour with the Witkowskis. It showed them that I had friends and could move freely.

When I moved into number seven it was easy to see that the Witkowskis' ground floor flat had been occupied by Jews. At the entrance the mezuzah* was still nailed; Witkowski had not even bothered to remove it. A small statue of the Virgin Mary now stood on a small table between the two windows of the main room, while the table was covered with a small white cloth on which was embroidered in Hebrew, "Remember The Sabbath Day to Keep It Holy"! For Witkowski all that mattered was that the Virgin should stand on a clean white cloth. He neither cared about, nor noticed, the embroidered letters.

The grinding poverty of the flat was a new and unpleasant experience, but I had to adapt myself to the family's way of life and to talk and think as they did in order to integrate successfully. I need hardly add that cleanliness was unknown. It was hard to sleep at night because of the bugs and fleas, but they were part of

---

* Parchment in a metal container on which is inscribed the first two paragraphs of the *Shema*, a Hebrew prayer. It is affixed to the doorposts in a Jewish home.

the general filth and not, I suspect, a legacy from the former tenants. I left the flat every day at seven in the morning, pretending to go to work, and came back in the evening, a few minutes before curfew, at seven. When I was really working at the shop at 113, Czerniakowska Street, for example, or as a businessman at 18, Nowoniarska Street, my days were occupied, but when I had no job, time dragged. What to do with it was a great problem. Just roaming around the streets was dangerous. It was easy enough to be arrested as a Pole but easier still as a suspected Jew. The easiest way in which to fill the hours was to visit the various churches in the Old City. I became fluent in Catholic liturgy and knew church customs and religious music well; I even got to know the priests of St. Franciscan, St. Yacek and the Capucine Church, as well as the Jesuits. It appeared that the great Jewish catastrophe had not as much as disturbed the even tenor of these lives. Not a ripple had marred the surface. It might have happened on another planet.

The Church had always been a very strong factor in Polish social and cultural life. And it had become much stronger in these wartime years of suffering and slavery; its influence was now more powerful than that of any underground political organisation. One might have expected some hints from the priests in their sermons, at least in general terms, about the iniquity of the crimes against their neighbours; but on the whole the official attitude was silence.

Mr. Witkowski was delighted with me. I went to church with him every Sunday, had a drink with him after Mass and listened patiently to all his tales. He thought Hitler was a great fool. He asked me, "Why did he put the Jews into a ghetto? This only led to an uprising which ruined half our city. If Hitler had had any sense he would have kept the Jews herded together on some open waste ground and we could have had their undamaged property."

Every new tenant who came to live in a block of flats had to be registered with the local authority via the porter. I hung on for weeks, afraid of seeing the porter or to be seen by him. One day Mrs. Witkowski told me that nowadays no one was allowed to live anywhere without being registered because one never knew— some idiot of a Jew might try and hide out. I went hot and cold, but agreed quietly that one had to be careful, that sort of thing could conceivably happen. The following morning I registered without mishap. Soon after this, trouble started again. One day, Witkowski told me that the porter had "discovered" three Jews and reported them to the Germans, and they had all been shot on the spot. The story filled me with fear, but I stayed on.

Every evening in summer the tenants organised evensong in the courtyard after curfew. Practically everyone joined in. Witkowski pressed me to join them. I, however, would not go, mainly because I wanted no contact with the murderous porter. Suddenly, to my surprise, I somehow became aware of other Jews hiding in the house. Some were even acquaintances of mine. I saw one of my former students who now lived in a flat above me, and a young man called Gutgisser whom I had known before the war. I noticed that he often went into the porter's flat. This alarmed me and I took good care to avoid him. Were they in league?

When the Polish Uprising of 1944 began, Witkowski was most annoyed. Why should Poles campaign against the Germans just now? Though the early fights in the Old City were successful for the Polish combatants, he felt that the Poles would be defeated and that catastrophe loomed large. He explained that this sort of revolt was foolhardy. It might be all right for Jews—who got their deserts. But surely Poles could be expected to act in a more sensible fashion.

Shortly afterwards, the mystery of number seven with its collaborating porter and its high Jewish population was cleared up. Next time the porter saw me, he shook my hand warmly and said we should have a drink to celebrate the Polish Uprising. When I refused he told me the whole story. "Of course I know you are a Jew; all your former pupils in this house have told me that you were their teacher. You were lucky that you found a place to lodge at number seven. In the other houses round here your life would have been worth nothing if the tenants had seen you living with a type like Witkowski! They would have smelt a rat at once." It turned out that some of the tenants were part of a huge conspiracy. The block housed an illegal printing press for an underground news sheet; ammunition was stored here; many

Poles who were politically suspect lived here; and so Jews could the more easily be hidden. The story about the three Jews discovered by the porter was deliberately allowed to circulate; it was a fabrication which helped to avert suspicion.

The porter was an active member of the underground, as it turned out. He wore a long beard, carried two pistols in his belt and had a string of grenades round his neck. His appearance terrified all who saw him. He looked like an old Viking or a twentieth-century Samson, who fought ceaselessly for about eight days and died in battle against the Germans in the streets of the Old City. He was one of the great heroes of the Uprising.

Jan Witkowski was totally ignorant of everything that was hidden, or being planned, or going on in number seven. He died of starvation during the Uprising, bitter and at odds with everyone. I must, however, admit that this odd character had many good points. It would be unjust to describe him as basically anti-semitic. His remarks about Jews or the ghetto were a rehash of what he had heard around him—and that sort of attitude was characteristic of the times he lived in. He was quite incapable of any original thought—even positively loving or positively hating were emotions unknown to him.

27. A Sunday Mass

EVERY SUNDAY MORNING, Witkowski took good care that I accompanied him—to Franciscan Church one Sunday, and to St. Yacek the next. Although Witkowski appeared to be a most observant Catholic, I felt that the drinks after the service were of equal, if not greater, importance to him. Every Saturday night he used to prepare the alcohol himself in readiness for Sunday. I, however, used to pay for it—this was the least that a humble useless lodger could do.

There was talk in the neighbourhood that the Germans were beginning to arrest people as they came out of church—they never came inside. They started the arrests because groups of young people often distributed some illegal newspapers to the worshippers as they came in and out. Even in the church, news sheets somehow filtered into missals and hymnals. I, among others, found these sheets a few times and eagerly collected them to devour later at home. They were my contact with the free, outside world. Yet the Gestapo knew that all this was taking place under their noses and the danger increased.

It was a sunny Sunday after breakfast and Witkowski and I were ready to go to Mass at St. Yacek Church in Freta Street. The church afforded me a place of shelter, but there were two aspects of Catholic worship that I struggled to avoid, though Witkowski pressed me continuously. I shrank from communion and confession. Now, I sensed a new danger—the Gestapo standing watching everyone as they came out of church. I asked my landlord very gently if we could stay at home, just this once? We could, after all, have our drinks as we always did. I gave him no reason for my request, but he realised at once that I was afraid of the Germans. He was silent for a few minutes. His wife, who had been listening, agreed with me that it would be better to stay at home. Though he had listened to me quietly enough he sprang up enraged as soon as he heard his wife speak. He shouted, "What! Us afraid of Jerries? I hope they all rot! Only Jews are afraid. We are not cowards!" And turning to me, "Come on, we're going! St. Anthony is our patron saint, and no Jerry would have the nerve to come into church." I felt half dead but had to pretend to be heroic and to agree with everything my landlord said. I said, "Fear? Of course we are not afraid. If you want to go, I'll accompany you."

Many people in festive mood were walking towards the church. We joined the throng walking along Sapiezynska towards Franciscan Street. I could not help noticing the stark ruins of the ghetto as we ambled along on this bright morning. As we approached St. Yacek, my thoughts sank deeper and deeper into that Jewish world that had vanished. Suddenly Witkowski turned towards the ruins, pointed and said, "You see, our God is powerful. He has given the Jews their due!" I remained silent.

The church was packed. The priest had started celebrating Mass; the choir sang and the organ played. I was long familiar with the prayers and the tunes, while I found the Latin easy to follow and mentally compared it with the Hebrew prayer books, since portions of the Latin are a direct transcription from some Hebrew texts. Of course, some aspects of the service were strange to me, such as the sprinkling with holy water and the sweet smell of the incense. But the hymns, the psalms and the lesson from the Old Testament were friendly and familiar. It was enough for me to close my eyes and follow word for word in Hebrew.

I sat next to Witkowski in the same pew. He, eyes closed, mumbled constantly and told his beads, kissing them intermittently. The priest mounted the pulpit to deliver his sermon in sudden silence. I glanced again at Witkowski while the sermon was in progress. His eyes were shut; I was completely forgotten. Suddenly there was a movement in the body of the church. Something had happened. The whisper passed from one to the other, "Germans have arrived and have mounted guard over the main door." Tension and nervousness grew among the worshippers. I realised that I was lost—the only Jew in the church, probably.

The priest stood firm and continued with his sermon but no one listened. People did not know what to do next. I looked again at Witkowski and saw to my horror that he was deathly pale and shaking like a leaf, fidgeting all the time. So now I had to be the hero! "Keep calm," I said to him, "they cannot come into the church. St. Anthony will protect us."

We were desperate. The Germans were lined up outside and waiting. The priest finished his sermon but stayed in his pulpit and asked all the worshippers to start singing hymns. Everybody joined in lustily but kept throwing nervous glances at the door. While this was going on, I noticed the young people, who were in the greatest danger, slipping out through a side door which led into another street. I realised at once what was happening, grabbed hold of Witkowski and moved with him towards the same side exit. He went on singing all the time, but after every few words threw in a favourite curse of his, damning the Germans.

Back home, when we had our drinks in our hands, Witkowski addressed me with pride, "I told you this morning—keep calm and don't be afraid of those Jerries; God is with us."

28. I Become a Salesman

ANY JEW WHO, after doubts and deliberations, left the ghetto for the Aryan side, could do so only if two conditions were satisfied. First, he had to have friends outside, and had to pay for shelter and food for himself and his family. The most incorrigible optimist could see no hopeful future in 1942. No one knew how long he would have to stay in hiding and pay dearly for his hellish existence.

Of course it was hardest of all for those Jews who, because of their semitic appearance and poor command of Polish, had to remain in hiding all the time and could not venture out. They were utterly dependent on the good will and humour of their shelterers, who had a great deal of say in what happened to them. Even these, however, were often driven to escape from their claustrophobic existence. Some posed as deaf mutes to avoid betraying themselves by speech deficiencies. They moved freely in the town, used sign language and even worked alongside Poles in various factories. This type of person often "heard" his workmates' and employers' opinion of the fate of Jews in Poland. Sometimes that fate evoked joy, sometimes sorrow.

There were others who found a "remedy" for their appearance by roaming the streets as professional chimney sweeps. They always carried brushes and ladders, wore black top hats, and, most important of all, smeared their faces thoroughly with soot. But those who fared best of all were the group who looked "Aryan" and spoke perfect Polish. My wife and I, happily, belonged to the latter category. Nevertheless, we would not have had the courage to leave the ghetto if we had not been in possession of sufficient funds to enable us to pay for survival for some little while. We did not consider that we would seriously have to set about earning a living and learning a trade. I never dreamt that I would end up as a salesman of black market goods, an illegal occupation punishable by death. This would have been dangerous even for a true Pole. It was rather ironic in my case, since I had been brought up in an environment where trade and manual work were rather looked down on and only the assiduous use of the intellect was cultivated.

We augmented our courage with a large sum of money. A very wealthy uncle of mine divided his fortune amongst his relatives on the day that the deportations started. He himself kept jewellery, gold and foreign currency, and was certain that with these he and his wife could survive anywhere. The shares he gave me were then worth half a million zlotys. He took his fortune to Treblinka; I took my shares to the Aryan side. Once outside, I gave them to a Polish friend and arranged with him that he would sell a few of them for me every month, to enable my wife and me to live. We also agreed that he should take a fixed sum for himself. I hoped that, in this way, we would be free from financial worries for some years. The first time I asked him to sell shares to the value of ten thousand zlotys, he told me that a terrible thing had happened. There were no more shares. I dared not ask too many questions. Incidents like this one were daily occurrences in Warsaw and often ended in tragedy. Money was appropriated, Jews were handed over to the Gestapo and so-called shelterers were rich and free from worry.

I listened calmly when my friend told me that there were "no shares", and merely said, in case he betrayed me to the police, that they had not been mine anyhow. In wartime everything seemed to be communal property! I hoped in this way to save my wife's life and my own, and did so. The man knew our whereabouts throughout the war, and never once did he betray us. At the time of the "New Order", the German occupation and mass murder, this Pole must be counted amongst the most decent of men in spite of the loss of the shares. I bear him no ill will. It turned out that he lost the whole lot in a German casino in Warsaw.

It was over and done with—but we were penniless. We now had to find ways of staying alive. My wife was always hidden with people who knew she was Jewish and I paid large sums for her keep. I lived openly as a Pole, moving freely and indulging in petty buying and selling, and had to earn enough to pay for necessities for both of us. I often sold things that no true Pole would have touched.

Drunkenness was common among Poles during the war. Everyone who could, drank, and there were many illicit stills. The vodka produced in this way was referred to as "bimber". The drink was secretly bottled and had an official seal attached, and was then sold openly. One of my Polish friends had an illicit still and I acted as wholesaler between him and the town stores. It was very dangerous but the pay was reasonable. Another black market commodity was saccharine. This, too, was secretly manufactured and enjoyed great popularity. It was much cheaper than the saccharine officially supplied to shops by the authorities. I also sold this and for some time was the main supplier to a group of shops in the Old City. Candles smuggled from Czechoslovakia were also my speciality. They came in such vast quantities and were of such good quality that business was brisk and profits high. I even managed to turn my landlord Witkowski into a businessman. He went daily to collect a supply of candles from the wholesaler and returned home at night with what was, for him, a colossal sum of money.

I also dealt in stolen sugar which officials from a central depot somehow spirited out by the sackful. I tried to sell all these articles at a very reasonable price and for a very small profit, since I did not want to become rich, just to survive. Because of this, the people to whom I sold were very sympathetic towards me. They regarded me as an "absent-minded intellectual" who was not orientated to the rough and tumble of war and its opportunities for getting rich quickly. These same shopkeepers who had taken over former Jewish-owned shops were themselves ruthless and extortionate towards their customers. Prices varied from day to day and they often made enormous profits. Not one of my clients ever dreamed that I was a Jew. My mobility and my dealing in black market goods was all the proof they needed that I was not connected with Jews. No Jew would have risked it.

My business transactions continued till a few weeks before the

Polish Uprising. There was a church in Senatorska Street called St. Anthony's, with a long, cloistered entrance. In the spring of 1944 things got difficult for me around the streets of the Old City and I decided that the church in Senatorska Street might, in time, be a safe hiding place since its entrance was some way from the street. I visited the place often, became well known to the priests, and felt quite at home within its walls. Apart from this, I became friendly with one of the servers, who had a kiosk outside the church in which he sold religious tracts and rosaries. He was an elderly bachelor, somewhat eccentric, and he kept me supplied with a stream of gossip about the priests and the congregation. He also told me all about his kiosk trade. These stories were told me over a cup of tea in his one-room flat near the church. The place terrified me. The walls were completely covered with pictures depicting New Testament scenes in lurid colours. Among them hung black crosses, large and small. The room, never cleaned, was thick with grime and the murky dampness was festooned with cobwebs. It was a nightmare.

I thought of one thing only. How marvellous it would be if I could take over the kiosk and sit inside with only my face showing. I learned from him that he had a sister who lived some distance away. He wanted to visit her, but was afraid to leave his business. I was overjoyed. We arranged that I would deputise for him whenever he wanted me to. Thus, in the spring of 1944, I learned a new trade; I sold crosses, missals, religious pictures and statues. Customers were few but I was anxious to impress my employer so, whenever he was away, I took a few crosses and other articles and pocketed them. When he returned I gave him a list of what I had really sold and what I had pocketed and asked him to work out how much money there should be in the till. He knew that I never remembered the cost of any article, so I always gave him out of my pocket the sum he stated. In terms of safety it was worth anything.

But everything must end. In June, 1944, I was sitting in the kiosk, looking out into the street and watching the people coming to and from the church. Suddenly, everyone scattered, gunfire burst forth, and the Germans were everywhere. It was dangerous and pointless to remain in the kiosk. I left hurriedly, ran into the church and with the few worshippers who were there I slipped out by a side door. I never dared go back to the church, and never found out what happened to the kiosk or its owner. The stormy days of the Uprising were drawing close. They marked the end of my career as a salesman.

29. Warsaw Without Jews

IT WAS SUMMER, 1943. Warsaw, which before the war had the largest Jewish community of some 350,000 and during the war about half a million, had now, after the Ghetto Uprising, officially no Jews at all. It was, as the Germans said, *Judenrein*. The only silent witness to this erstwhile community was—until May, 1943 —the large Tlomackie Synagogue. It had remained undamaged because it was not in the ghetto. It stood shuttered, silent and secretive, as if shrouded in deep melancholy.

It was obvious to all that even this solitary symbol would disappear in time—and it did, after the Ghetto Uprising had sub-sided. I was out in the street and saw what happened to the Tlomackie Synagogue. One sunny morning, two SS vans drove up, sealed off the surrounding streets and blew it up with dyna-mite. All that was left was a mound of rubble. The detonation caused a great deal of blast damage in the neighbourhood and the pavements were covered with broken glass. Their job done, the SS left happily, hoping that the pile of debris would convince everybody that the Jews of Warsaw were no more. Their next plan was to clear away the ruins of the ghetto and lay out a park in the area, to be called the Adolf Hitler Park. To this end the Germans brought in hundreds of Jews from other countries to remove the ruins and prepare the site. Work continued for over a year. The detonations required to demolish the empty shells of buildings could be heard all over Warsaw, and people who lived nearby looked with horror at the clearance programme inside the ghetto walls. The Polish Uprising of 1944 put a sudden end to the work; the Germans left the ghetto in a hurry, and many Jews doing forced labour were freed by the Polish fighters. There was never a Hitler Park in Warsaw.

It was said that there were no Jews and no symbols of Jewishness in Warsaw. But for those of us who had survived, the streets of the city were filled not only with memories of the past, but with actual objects freely seen, identified and sold. There were Jewish books that had belonged to libraries and private collections. The pages were used for wrapping goods in shops, as there was a great shortage of paper. Former Jewish-occupied flats were now in the possession of Polish tenants, and their specifically Jewish contents used to light fires. Wood and coal were in short supply too, and every day my landlord brought home sacks of Jewish books which he burned in the stove. He pointed out that the Jewish religion was going up in smoke.

In all the market places there was a brisk sale of long woollen prayer shawls—*tallisim*. Wool was scarce and these articles had great value. The large prayer shawls were the right size for a woman's dress, so they were dyed and, when remade, bore no resemblance to the original article. Pious women were seen in the church in these smart new outfits.

A different value was placed on the scrolls of the law. They had multiple uses and were sold by the yard. Shoemakers bought them for inner linings, hat-makers acquired them, and so did other groups of artisans. In the market places the scrolls could be seen lying in the mud with heaps of junk. There were some literary and intelligent connoisseurs who concealed a whole scroll in their homes. They felt that the time would come, after the war, when it would fetch a good price.

In the Old City, I often visited a provision shop whose owner was drunk half the time. He was hardly concerned about his business. One day he called me aside to whisper something to me. He wanted to sell me a scroll which he described as a "Torah"— using the Hebrew word. The proceeds of the sale were, of course, to buy drink. He said his daughter had been given the scroll by a

German in return for one kilo of sausages. He had it in his house, he said, winking broadly at me at the same time. His wife, who had heard the conversation, yelled out at this point, "Don't listen to him. He is a fool and a drunkard." I left the shop frightened and never went there again. Obviously they both knew who I really was.

A sad fate also awaited the synagogical silver objects associated with traditional Judaism. Shops in every street were selling them off and they were also on free display in the markets: goblets, candlesticks, scroll decorations, spice boxes and money boxes. They had once been the proud possessions of countless Jewish homes, used and displayed at feasts and festivals. They were now being sold for next to nothing but customers were scarce. In time of war these were luxury items, unlike wool and paper.

Thousands of former Jewish flats still had the mezuzahs nailed up on the doorposts. The new owners did not even bother to remove this sole relic of destruction. There were no more Jews, but the symbols of Judaism were everywhere.

Jews in hiding often met by chance in the streets, restaurants and churches. In Sewerynow Street you would find the Catholic Community Centre of St. Joseph, which had a well-patronised restaurant. The fact that it was in a quiet side street and that the service by nuns was so pleasant attracted many Jews to the place. They came there for lunch and to meet friends, both Jews and Gentiles. It was known to nearly all Jews hidden in Warsaw, and offered an hour's respite from the cruel outside. The atmosphere was peaceful; everyone knew everyone else and fear was temporarily at bay. I went to the restaurant every day for more than a year. On principle I avoided those whom I suspected of being Jewish; I always tried to sit with Poles. It turned out that these so very Catholic Poles were, in fact, Jews. Among the diners I often saw previous friends and pupils of mine. We glanced at each other but conversation was out of the question.

There was one diner who always attracted particular attention; a heavily-veiled woman in black who always wore widow's weeds. No one ever saw her face. The heavy mourning garb, which she wore in summer and winter, and the thick veil were symbols of some great tragedy—and I was certain that she was Jewish too. One day I asked a fellow diner who she was. He told me she was Mrs. Basia Berman, the wife of the active Jewish underground worker Adolf Berman. She acted well, and sometimes overacted, the part of a veiled Catholic.

Again, Jews were one of the main topics of conversation in the streets, markets, public houses and shops. They were discussed with callousness, often with hate; even as a scourge that had to be wiped out. The Germans were continuing to churn out propaganda inciting the Poles to hatred of the Jews. They exploited the murder of Polish officers at Katyn, saying they were killed by Jews in Russia. Suddenly leaflets were distributed in Warsaw describing the "ritual murders" of the Middle Ages, when Jews were supposed to have killed Christian children for their Passover feast. These tales were lavishly illustrated. It seemed that the Germans were trying to justify their criminal actions. It is not surprising that such propaganda poisoned the minds of many people, even when those against whom it was directed had disappeared.

An incident in the Old City demonstrates this point well. Two German officers were shot by the Polish Underground in broad daylight. I saw the two dead men lying in Freta Street. As if by pre-arranged design, everyone in the vicinity was heard saying that the Jews had done it.

I looked at the relics of what had been, listened to the things which made a mockery of human intelligence, and had to remain silent.

30. Death on the Aryan Side

EVERY JEW who escaped from the ghetto was moved by two emotions; joy at leaving certain death behind and fear of the future. On the Aryan side he suffered indescribable torment, as he was afraid of being caught both as a Jew and as a Pole—for so many of the latter were also wantonly shot.

Being ill presented great difficulty. The Jew avoided telling his Catholic neighbours anything about his sickness and often walked around with high fever and pain, afraid of reporting this as it might cost him the roof over his head. Going to a doctor meant trusting a stranger with your guilty secret—that you were a Jew. And if you did risk it and disease was diagnosed and admission to hospital for an operation suggested, a new set of problems arose, and the associated dangers were even greater. Reporting the presence of Jewish patients in hospital to the Germans was not unknown, and of course their fate was sealed. In Warsaw, many Jewish patients were shot. In short, very many Jews died on the Aryan side. It is a little-known fact.

If a Jew died, who was there to arrange a funeral or even to inform the priest? For the Jews lived alone, avoiding contact even with members of their families who might be in a similar position. Occasionally, when a Jew who passed as a Pole died, the neighbours would, as an act of charity, arrange for the priest to administer the last rites, buy the coffin and give him a traditional Catholic burial. We heard of these funerals after the war, when relatives came to enquire about the fate of some members of their family.

It was totally different when one of the "hidden" Jews died since, officially, their existence was completely unknown. The Poles who secretly kept an eye on them were terrified that someone should find out and report them to the Germans. The penalty was death. So they just did not know how to dispose of the corpse. Doubtless there were many funerals of the "hidden" ones, but how they were managed is a mystery. I know of one case, however; that of a friend of mine, a famous pre-war store-owner in Warsaw called Rivele Rottenberg. His linen shop on Gensia Street was very well-known to all Polish Jews. Parents felt it a privilege to buy trousseaux there for their children. Rivele Rottenberg knew how to handle his customers and saw them to the door with the traditional wishes of happiness and good health.

When the Germans occupied Warsaw, Jewish stores were broken into and plundered, especially those on Gensia Street. Rottenberg's long-established one was stripped bare by the invaders. A rumour was heard that the owner, in despair, had committed suicide, but this was far from true. He remained the same smiling optimist as ever and even instilled confidence into his fearful neighbours, since he was certain that the Jewish people would survive.

The Rottenberg family were very well known in the ghetto. One of the sons did a great deal of welfare work and, until the ghetto was finally liquidated, was assistant to Emanuel Ringelblum, the famous historian. The Rottenbergs looked after Rivele with great care as he was an old man, and typhus was spreading in epidemic proportions.

I often met the old man, especially in the summer of 1942, when he came to visit the private school on Nowolipki Street nearly every day. He would sit in the class after school and crack jokes at the expense of the Germans. His appearance was always affluent and cheerful; his beard neatly trimmed, his collar white and the traditional caftan clean and neat. He used to say that the caftan had been adopted by Jews to hide their patched and tattered trousers. . . .

When the deportations started, the Rottenberg family tried to find a home on the Aryan side where they could hide their old father. This was difficult as he looked very Jewish, but a place was found and he was smuggled out and handed over to his new guardians, who were prepared to look after him for a stated monthly payment. The children, of course, were overjoyed, but not for long. In a short time Rivele fell ill and news of his death reached the ghetto. The Polish family telephoned the Rottenbergs asking for money for the funeral expenses. Money was sent via the working groups, but we heard that it was used for alcohol to drown their own sorrows and that the poor old man was still in the house unburied. A new sum was despatched—a number of times. The guardians seemed in no hurry to rid themselves of the corpse. There were, of course, problems connected with this sort of funeral, but a solution was found. The Polish house was near the Vistula. After curfew, with the corpse tied in a sack, they slipped out of the house and threw it into the river. In a few days the body was washed up on the bank and was found by a Polish policeman. He had often visited the Rottenberg shop before the war and recognised the corpse at once. He had it taken to the nearest Catholic cemetery and interred there.

By an odd quirk of fate, a granddaughter of the old man heard the story later. She was living as a Pole and was sent to a public house to buy some beer. A group of policemen were drinking and talking about the incident: this is how she learned of her grandfather's end.

31. The Penitent

THE INCIDENT in St. Yacek's Church when the SS-men surrounded it was not sufficiently disturbing to keep me away altogether. I felt that it was safer to be in the church during the day, especially when services were in progress. Something else happened in that same church one Sunday; something rather memorable.

In one of the narrow streets in the Old City of Warsaw there was a poor tumbledown cottage, containing a small shop at the front and one room at the back. The owner of this business was an old lady of eighty who had no commercial sense whatsoever. She did not seem to know the price of goods in her shop and certainly had no idea how to give small change from a note of any denomination. Added to this, she was deaf. All these faults were virtues in my eyes and I liked her enormously. I became a frequent customer. I had no anxiety about going there, as the old lady was far from comprehending current problems, particularly those which troubled Jews in hiding. She sold bread, butter and other provisions.

Every morning after leaving No. 7, Sapiezynska Street in the same neighbourhood, I used to go there for breakfast. We had come to an arrangement by which I bought the articles and she would make tea for me. I was her best customer, and it was the first visit of my day. These visits gradually lengthened and I finally used to spend some two hours with her. We became very friendly and I listened patiently to all her stories. She complained a great deal of her loneliness and of her great age, which was a curse to her as she was becoming less mobile. She also told me of her only son whom the Germans had deported because he had been a member of the Polish Underground. Her daughter-in-law, who lived in Warsaw, was, she said, utterly worthless. From the time of her husband's deportation she had been running around with Germans and was making a big profit out of this activity. The old lady trusted me as a close friend, since I was such a patient and interested listener.

This small, narrow street was nearly always deserted. Movement was minimal, much to my delight. Sitting in the little shack, I would glance frequently at the street to see if anything was happening. A few times I saw a number of familiar faces from the ghetto, among them the well-known resister Dr. Adolf Berman. I was distressed to see him, and concerned for his safety. He trotted briskly along with a paper folder under his arm, keeping well to the side of the wall. This behaviour was hazardous. It was obvious that he was none too happy in his position. I often wanted to tell him to change his way of walking in the street, but I was afraid of scaring him even more.

During my breakfast, various people would come into the shop and the old lady always told me who they were. One day a fellow came in and bought nothing, but spent some time in conversation with her, asking about business, relatives and neighbours, and how her health was. I went on eating and pretended not to listen. I could not help noticing, however, that he was watching me, scrutinising me up and down in fact. His looks radiated suspicion. When he left the shop, the old woman told me that he was a relation of hers and one had to beware of him, since he was on the lookout for someone to blackmail. He was completely rotten and had many murders on his conscience. My heart sank. It was my last visit to the old lady, but the face of her relation was well imprinted on my memory. I saw him often in the streets of the Old City, and confirmed that he was an informer and a well-known finder of Jews, whom he handed over personally. Walking the streets, I often thought of him and dreaded any direct contact. When I did see him, I hid speedily.

One Sunday, at the end of summer 1943, I was again sitting in

St. Yacek's Church in Freta Street with Witkowski. After Mass, as we were leaving with a crowd of worshippers, I suddenly noticed a figure lying prone on the floor, arms outstretched in the form of a cross. He lay in a side chapel, prostrated before an altar dedicated to a saint. I had never seen any living person in this position, only pictures of Jesus crucified. A feeling of horror ran through me and yet I was intrigued. I said nothing to Witkowski, but went on home with him and had the Sunday drink and lunch afterwards. All the time I thought about the man lying face downwards in the church. By the afternoon I could contain myself no longer, but had to go back to see if he was still there.

The church was silent as the grave. There were a few people kneeling in private prayer. The man who repented still lay there motionless before the altar of the saint. Suddenly I realised, with a shudder, that the still figure was none other than the informer whom I so carefully avoided and who was responsible for so many Jewish deaths. I was perhaps fortunate in thinking that now he was regretting all he had done. Perhaps he saw the evil of his ways and was seeking a way back to a state of grace? How mistaken I was! In subsequent months I learned that in respect of Jews he had not changed; he was as ruthless as ever in his pursuit of them. I heard him talked about in various quarters and continued to avoid him like the plague. He probably felt that any atrocity committed against Jews did not contravene his religious principles, and he seemed not to realise that he needed to seek the path of repentance and forgiveness for this evil too. It often struck me, too, that had one of the saintly disciples, before whom he lay prostrate, come down amongst us, he would have been the first to inform the Germans about a Jew. . . .

32. Zygmunt the Cripple

I OFTEN WONDERED what happened to Jews who hid in the woods. And what about those in concentration camps and other ghettos? But perhaps those who acted out the tragi-comedy of being Poles and Catholics suffered most. It is hard to imagine the life of such a Jew, mixing freely with everybody, and being easily rebuffed by the expressions on people's faces; above all the constant role-playing, like an actor in some old classic play. I say constant, for one continued to act even at night. One groan, one word spoken in sleep would have betrayed the Jew. The smallest error of judgement in movement or in speech led to death.

These were my thoughts after a harrowing experience in the district of Czerniakow. It occurred in the main thoroughfare, Czerniakowska Street. In the summer of 1943, after the Ghetto Uprising, I again had to return to living with my secret in Czerniakow. I worked at 113, Czerniakowska Street, in a shop which sold spirits and provisions, owned by an elderly man, an engineer called Kantorski. I knew the shop well when my wife I and were living in the house on the common; I went there a number of times to buy various articles of food. Kantorski lived in Zyrardow, just outside Warsaw, and he travelled in daily. I often chatted with him and felt that, as a patriotic Pole, he could be trusted.

After my experiences at Skolimow and Chylice, I remembered this man and the trust I had put in his patriotism. The days were long, bitter and empty, and so I thought I might try to get a job as a salesman. I prepared a story for him. It was that I was a Polish officer in extreme difficulties in Warsaw, a deserter from the army who had refused to register with the Germans. I had come from Poznan and was now desperate for work. Of course, the whole business of tricking him was very risky, apart from the fact that the area was notorious for the thieves, hooligans and other delinquents who roamed around.

When Kantorski was alone in his shop I told him my tale in confidence and asked if he needed someone to help him. He was very sympathetic to my story and, as a patriot, felt he should employ me. However, he made one condition. He wanted a cooked lunch, to be prepared daily in the room behind the shop. He felt this would suit both of us. Smilingly, I readily agreed, saying, "This is indeed divine providence. Before the war, when I was in the army, I was a chef and head of the Army Catering

Corps." In reality, I had no clue as to how one set about preparing a meal. I just relied on my memories of the taste of food and the sight of my mother cooking at home when I was a child, and the hope that some miracle would happen.

Kantorski never for one second suspected that I was a Jew. The way I spoke, my military bearing, and the confidence with which I had expressed myself were far from Jewish traits at that time. I started work, taking care to avoid talking about Jews, not only with him but with the customers who came to the shop. Friends of my employers often came in. They were mainly journalists, writers and former civil servants who all cursed the Nazis. But one often heard, too, that the one good thing the Germans had done was to rid Poland of its Jews, and for this one should be grateful. Incidentally, this was also the opinion of Mr. Kantorski. I need not say how I felt in the company of these people. I was always silent and never entered into any discussion, but did my work diligently and my employer was very pleased with me, since profits rose and the business was thriving.

Mr. Kantorski was also pleased with my cooking and said the lunches I prepared were better than those he got at home. I cooked the things I knew and liked: pea soup, fruit soup and steaks. There was no need to cook ham and pork, for apart from the fact that I did not know how, he did not ask for it. I made chopped farfel soup which delighted Mr. Kantorski and he always said, "Where did you learn to make such wonderful savoury dishes?" In the end, he said he must bring his wife and daughter to one of my lunches, so that they too could learn about good food. They came, ate and asked for recipes. After this event, I took the liberty of asking Mr. Kantorski if I could invite a friend of mine and he consented gladly. Thus, on one solitary occasion, my wife, acting the complete Catholic stranger, dined with us.

All would have been well, but the summer sun and the long light days were my enemies. Twenty-four hours of uninterrupted night would have been paradise. The streets were filled with layabouts who, in these days of war, were having great success at earning money without working: overfed drunkards who cared for no one, and revelled in the situation. They awaited any odd

German troops in the burning city of Warsaw

Yitzhak Cukierman, Anielewicz's second in command. He survived and now lives in Israel

Mordechai Anielewicz, leader of the ghetto uprising. After three weeks of fighting, in May 1943, the Germans surrounded his bunker; he gave his mother poison and he and his comrades committed suicide

Fighters in the Warsaw ghetto

turn of events which they could use to their advantage. I feared them constantly. The leader of the gang was a one-legged man who called himself Zygmunt. He spent an hour or two every day selling the Nazi paper *Nowy Kurier Warszawski* and hung around the streets the rest of the time, the spokesman for the crooks. He and his friends had an off-licence they always used and did their drinking there. They never came to "our" shop.

I always tried to keep off the streets. Eventually, I used to spend the night in the shop without the boss's knowledge. I slept on the stone floor, and managed cautiously to open the shop in the morning and lock up at night without his guessing that I stayed there. I was terrified of falling into the hands of the street gangs. My luck lasted for eight weeks: then, one afternoon, it happened. I went out of the shop—and bumped into Zygmunt. He just looked at me and that was enough to make me quake. We went our separate ways. But that night in the shop was sleepless for me.

The next day I saw Zygmunt limping towards the shop. He came in, greeted us and asked for half a bottle of vodka. I was busy with other customers, so Mr. Kantorski served him. I pretended not to see him. He stood there and, glancing in all directions, started to complain about present circumstances. At one time, he said, it was all different. When there were lots of Jews around, life was better, especially the year before they were put into the ghetto. His language was colourful. He remembered an old religious Jew coming out of the synagogue; there was snow everywhere, and he had thrashed the Jew soundly. The bright red of his blood had trickled across the white snow—this was his favourite picture. He even remembered the spot where the incident had occurred. Those were the days! But now, nothing like that came his way. My boss smiled and I did too. Zygmunt walked out.

My head was throbbing. What was the point of these stories of his? Was he getting at me? I met one of my Polish friends who knew of my true identity and asked his advice; he thought that it was idle chatter and I had nothing to fear. I thought otherwise, but what could I do? I had to stay put. The days passed and each seemed like eternity—till one warm August day when I was alone in the shop and noticed two men approaching—Zygmunt and an SS officer. They both came in and the officer asked for a bottle of vodka in German. I asked Zygmunt to translate. Both laughed and the SS man repeated the request in German. Another customer came in and I served her. While I was doing this, the German took out a camera and took a snap of me. I pretended to act stupidly and kept quiet.

The two men sat down at a table in the shop, ordered drinks and said I must have one as well. What next? I kept my head and Zygmunt said, "It's odd, all the kids in the street say this shop is owned by a Jew and we should boycott it." I replied, "The things kids say! They will say anything. They say you are a collaborator with the Gestapo." Zygmunt and the German looked at each other and did not know how to react to this. Zygmunt pressed on. He took a packet of pornographic pictures out of his pocket and showed them to me, one after the other. I fell in quickly. He knew that normally a Jew would shudder at this, but I carefully examined them all and expressed delight. I looked in my pocket and fished out a picture of myself taken in 1937 with a group of Poles. It had been taken while I was in hospital and the others, like myself, were all patients there. When Zygmunt saw it he screamed, "Here you look like a real Jew!" I pretended not to understand. A few of Zygmunt's friends, who had been waiting outside for something to happen, came in. They went into a whispered conference and I stood around, for all the world interested and attentive.

Zygmunt and the SS man got up and paid, and they all went out together. They were pretty sure I would not try to escape; they had assessed me accurately, and now simply needed the opportunity to finish me off. I stood alone in the shop but came to a decision fast. There was a back door leading into the yard. Slowly, I went out and stood quietly in the yard; there was a cabinet maker's factory there and the workers greeted me as I ambled past. It was a former Jewish prayer-house and I could see, through the open windows, the Hebrew inscriptions on the walls. In the street I caught a bus into town. I never returned to the street or the shop.

Later, when I risked 'phoning him and arranged a meeting in town, Mr. Kantorski told me what had happened afterwards. The day after I left, a car stopped outside his shop and two Gestapo men got out. They came into the shop with two sub-machine guns and arrested him, being quite certain that he was the Jew! He was searched and questioned for hours at the police station before they finally realised he was not the man they wanted. They also saw from the snap the SS man had taken that they were mistaken. When they asked him for my address, he did not know what to reply as I had carefully avoided giving him one. They released him, with one request: as soon as I reappeared in the shop, he was to let them know. He gave me one last piece of advice: never to come to Czerniakowska Street again.

33. In Search of Friends

AFTER THE MEETING with Zygmunt and the SS officer it was obvious that I could not go back to my old hiding place at 7, Sapiezynska Street. Gestapo headquarters had my name and my photograph and it was all too easy to find out my address. It merely required checking up with the Registration Department in the City. I therefore began to think about old friends and professional colleagues who, at this critical time, might be willing to shelter me for one or two nights at least. I had to bide my time somewhere to ascertain if the Germans would indeed seek out my address and go there to arrest me.

One sunny day I was walking along Marszalkowska Street to visit some Polish friends. As if miraculously, there appeared alongside me a priest, Father Jaskulowski, who had been a fellow teacher of mine at the Commercial High School in Prosta Street. I had not even thought about him when mentally compiling lists of friends. He and I had taught in that part of the school which was under the direction of Dr. Rudolf Taubenschlag, a famous Polish educationist and a considerable innovator. I had not been very friendly with Father Jaskulowski. His appearance and opinions had always created a gulf between us. Now, however, I was delighted to meet him.

I greeted him and we walked along as in pre-war days—the Catholic priest and the Jew in the streets of Warsaw in 1943! A truly historical moment! He smiled, but I could not interpret his expression. Was he glad to see me alive, or was he, as always, smiling and secretive in his attitude to Jews? I got to the point straight away. I informed him about our former Jewish colleagues. Rudolf Taubenschlag, I said, suffered from slow starvation and committed suicide when the deportations started. Szymon Lubelski was arrested early in the war and died soon afterwards. I felt that Father Jaskulowski was unmoved and indifferent. We walked on, and I told him about myself: that I was wanted by the Gestapo and was desperate for somewhere to spend the night. He was silent and his impassivity began to frighten me. Eventually he spoke. Regretfully, he could not help me, but where did I get the courage to walk so freely in this busy main street? The danger was great, especially for a man whose Jewishness could be proved so easily. He also tried to tell me that a tragedy of such magnitude as had overtaken the Jews was a complex problem and the reasons had to be carefully considered. We had, by now, reached St. Alexander's Church. This part of the street was absolutely packed with German officers, and in the bustle I made my farewells, thankful to leave the priest.

I thought of an address in the vicinity. It was the residence of another former colleague and his wife, Stefan and Wanda Zolkiewski. Both had taught literature and were broad-minded, friendly people, who had an excellent relationship with all the pupils, including the Jewish ones. When I got to the flat, Stefan was alone. I told him of the fate of our former Jewish colleagues and begged his help for a night or two. He could not do anything either. I was amazed to hear him say so, though of course there was no reason for being angry with him: what *did* surprise me was his nonchalant attitude to all I had said. I left as homeless as I had come.

The failures with the priest and with Stefan Zolkiewski affected me badly but I did not give up hope. I decided to risk another visit, to a woman whom I knew well, a former headmistress, Mrs. Maria Rosciszewska. Before the war she had been a member of the Polish National Democratic Party and had freely admitted to being antisemitic. I nevertheless hoped that she might in all humanity help me, and she did.

The way to her house was agonising for me, since she lived opposite the building which housed the SS, a Polish former student hostel. I ran up the stairs and knocked. She opened the door herself, in outdoor clothes, as she was just about to leave. Immediately she saw me she hurried me inside, and I knew at once that I was dealing with a person vastly different from the previous pair. She insisted that I had a meal and while I ate, she did not cease talking about the Jewish tragedy, about the Uprising in the ghetto; and she questioned me constantly about her former friends and students who had been interned there. She frequently posed the question—whoever could have envisaged such an outcome? Who could have foreseen that antisemitism would lead to mass murder? It was beyond comprehension. She mentioned the names Lutoslawski, Niemojewski, Dmowski, who had been former mentors of the doctrine of antisemitism in Poland. Had they known where their ideologies would lead, they would never have disseminated such propaganda. She believed that after the war, antisemitism would be a crime, in the legal sense, wherever it occurred. After the indifference I had encountered, her horror at the Jewish tragedy left me speechless. It was magic.

She was prepared to help me and my wife as much as she could, and immediately recommended a safe hideout for Henrietta. This was in St. Mary's Convent in Hoza Street, which already housed a number of Jewish children. She also promised financial aid and this actually continued until the Polish Uprising in 1944. It was particularly hard for her to help me, as she was intimately connected with the Polish underground movement. Her house was at their disposal, and as such was suspected by the Germans. Though I had no shelter, this visit had uplifted me: she had treated me as an equal. With renewed hope I decided to go on trying to look for a hideout.

I remembered another friend and told myself I would try once more. If this visit did not work, I would go back to 7, Sapiezynska Street and let events take their course.

In 1938, Professor M. Schor, a famous scholar and Rabbi, had introduced me to a senior civil servant from the Ministry of Culture and Religious Affairs in Warsaw, Stanislaw Piechowicz. I had met him a few times and was impressed by his liberal attitude. I had always remembered his address, 10, Senatorska Street, which was near the official residence of Dr. Fischer, the German Governor of Warsaw. Regardless of the danger, I decided to go and pay Mr. Piechowicz a visit. He listened carefully to my tale, sat some time in deep thought, then said, "Of course you can't go back and sleep at Sapiezynska Street. You must stay here for the night. Don't worry about tomorrow." His reply saved me—at least for one more night. It turned out that Stanislaw Piechowicz was also deeply committed to underground work, and the following morning he dealt with my problems quite simply. The next day, he said, I could return to Sapiezynska Street without fear. Friends of his who worked in the Registration Department had withdrawn my card and the Gestapo would be hard put to it to find me.

Piechowicz was a rare character. He visited me nearly every day at Sapiezynska Street and at subsequent hiding places, to show Witkowski and others who provided me with shelter that I had Polish friends. Witkowski was moved to tears. He was puffed up with pride that someone of that level of society should visit his house. The fact that Piechowicz was my friend also raised me in his esteem. Eventually he asked Mr. Piechowicz if he might be allowed to offer him a drink, and the three of us sat together, raising our glasses.

Maria Rosciszewska and Stanislaw Piechowicz are both dead. Mrs. Rosciszewska fell fighting in the Polish Uprising of 1944, and Piechowicz died shortly afterwards. I shall never forget them.

Added in London

Now, twenty odd years after these events, I should perhaps find some excuse for the behaviour of Stefan Zolkiewski. He was an active member of the illegal Polish Communist Party, and became a famous public figure and Cabinet Minister in Poland after the war. His political activities were unknown to me in 1943. It is possible that, because of them, he felt it imperative to avoid a former Jewish colleague. The British press referred to him frequently in the spring of 1968 in connection with the expulsion of well-known Poles from political and intellectual life. He was not, however, a Jew.

34. Zygmunt in 1945

THERE IS A POST-WAR SEQUEL to the Czerniakowska Street story and Zygmunt.

It was the winter of 1945–1946. I was again in Warsaw, working and busy, and one day I was hurrying to keep an appointment at the one undamaged hotel left, the Polonia in the centre of town, which had become a meeting place for visitors from all over the world. I was to meet Louis Segal, the General Secretary of the Jewish Labour Committee of the USA.

It was cold and frosty and snow covered the ruins of the city; it was just growing dark. There were plenty of people around and among them I suddenly saw, as if in a dream, a figure who reminded me of Zygmunt of Czerniakowska Street. I could hardly believe my own eyes. I stared—and it was indeed he, one-legged Zygmunt, quite unchanged. He stood in front of the hotel, chanting, "I buy old gold, golden coins, currency, etc." The tone was the same as when he had called out in 1943, "*Nowy Kurier Warszawski, Nowy Kurier Warszawski!*" The old horror flowed over me and in my mind's eye I saw his entry with the SS officer into Kantorski's shop; I remembered the verbal cat and mouse game. I was bewildered and did not know what to do, but I felt something had to be done now. A Polish army officer was walking by. Without thinking, I went up to him and said that the dealer in gold outside the hotel had been a German collaborator, and I asked him to request to see his identity card. I did not know the surname, but I asked him to look and see if his Christian name was Zygmunt. If it was, the officer should take him to the police station at once. The officer was most courteous and quietly asked to see the one-legged man's identity card. He looked at it, tucked it into the cuff of his coat and escorted Zygmunt to the police station which was in the same street. I followed at a distance, since I too would have to make a statement. The police officer in charge of the station asked to see my identity card, and then enquired why I had petitioned for the arrest of the other man. I quietly told him about the role that Zygmunt had played during the war. The officer listened gravely and said this was the concern of another special department whose head office was round the corner. He would dispatch Zygmunt and I was to walk round and ask for formal proceedings to be established. When I asked for the return of my identity card, he said it would be given back to me after some investigations had been made.

I did not particularly want to go with them to this special department that dealt with crimes like collaboration, so I went along alone. Zygmunt was escorted out by two plain-clothes men. It was only five minutes' walk. Arriving there, I sat and waited one, two hours. Still no sign of Zygmunt or the two policemen. After two and a half hours the detectives appeared alone, and blind drunk. They said I was under arrest! Two policemen on duty there asked why and they said, "Because he has accused an innocent man of crimes which he never committed." I summed up this farcical situation and I asked again for the return of my identity card, hoping to get out as quickly as possible. But they would not hear of it. They went on repeating drunkenly, "He must be arrested." The place was in an uproar so I demanded at the top of my voice to be taken to the head of the section. A senior officer appeared and asked what was happening. I begged him to give me a private interview so that I need not talk to him in front of the two detectives.

I told him the whole story of Czerniakowska Street and described the recent farce. Finally I asked again for the return of my card. The official got it back for me and, in my presence, severely

reprimanded the detectives. He promised me that he would have
Zygmunt arrested that evening and requested that I come in the
morning to present the facts to him. I was there in good time,
waiting for Zygmunt to be brought in. When they did bring a
prisoner in he was a complete stranger to me. He had both legs
and was not in any way connected with my story. It seemed to
me that the two detectives were having their own back on me,
and that anyhow Zygmunt had bribed them well. The senior
officer lost his temper and warned the detectives that if they did
not produce Zygmunt they would have cause to regret it. He asked
me to telephone the following morning and said that when he had
Zygmunt there, he would ask me to come again.

I telephoned a number of times and was always given a muddled
noncommittal answer. After a few days, the official told me that
the matter was out of his hands. All he could do was to give me
Zygmunt's address and, if I wished to follow the matter up, I
could get in touch with the Public Prosecutor. I thought long and
seriously and finally decided the whole thing was best left alone.

Zygmunt went on plying his trade in front of the Polonia hotel
and I avoided him like the plague. I began to feel afraid of him
again, and also of the two detectives whom I often saw in the
street. Whenever I saw them, I hid in a doorway. I was auto-
matically repeating the pattern of the occupation.

35. The Ghetto Walls

WITH Skolimow, Chylice and Czerniakow behind me, I soldiered
on for all the world as if nothing had happened. I had always
wondered how human beings had the strength to fight so desperately for mere existence. Then I realised why. I thought: perhaps *I* would be the one to escape from hell. I am sure that others
living as I did thought the same. From this hope I derived courage
and the will to survive. I went on living in my hideout at Sapiezynska Street, coming in just before curfew and departing early

in the morning to go to my non-existent job. But the days dragged interminably, the summer days especially; they were long and light and proved a rather tricky problem. How marvellous it would have been if one of the Egyptian plagues had descended and darkness had permanently enveloped the land!

A minor miracle happened. I had begun to frequent a grocer's shop at 18, Nowiniarska Street, near Francisan Street. The whole of Nowiniarska Street ran parallel with the ghetto wall and the street was nearly always empty. At first I bought a few small articles of food and tried to get acquainted with the shopkeeper. He made a very good impression on me. The shop, too, was somehow different from all the others in the neighbourhood; it was clean and neat, the service was courteous and there was no overcharging. After a while, I had got to know quite a lot about the owner of the shop. His name was Ignacy Pulawski. He came from East Poland, and had been a member of the Polish Upper House (*Senat*) before the war; he now lived "illegally" in Warsaw, since as a politician he was in danger of arrest by the Germans.

As may be imagined, I trusted him implicitly, and confided some of my problems to him. I said that I too was wanted by the Germans, but never breathed a word about being a Jew. We became close friends and he kept nothing from me, giving me details of his life and all manner of information about the current situation gleaned from the illegal press and radio.

Pulawski had been in his shop at the time of the Ghetto Uprising, and actually witnessed everything that happened. He repeated the details constantly, cursing mankind for allowing such a tragedy to occur. As one Pole to another, he also told me about the behaviour of fellow Poles who came to gape at the horrors. It would be a permanent blot on the pages of Polish history, he said. He often expressed his political opinions while I, on principle, avoided such discussions. He was bitterly opposed to Stalin and always compared him with Hitler. I felt ill at ease; Hitler was the murderer of Jews, and the only hope for surviving Jews, we all thought, was the successful outcome of the Soviet campaigns.

In addition to selling provisions, Mr. Pulawski derived a large income from the sale of illegal sugar which he acquired from friends who worked in the Municipality. In time he and I went into partnership. He gave me sugar and I sold it to other shops and pastrycooks. I spent a few hours every day in his business and this partnership flourished for nearly a year. From the shop I was able to see everything that went on in the ghetto simply by looking over the outer wall. I saw a number of Jewish slave workers cleaning away the ruins, and the most modern machinery being used to expedite the work. Tracks were laid and wagonloads of bricks and metal driven out every day. All the work, machines and wagons came to a standstill as soon as the Polish Uprising started.

The subject of Jews was therefore freely discussed by customers in the shop. Occasionally, a certain German officer who came in to buy something would express his opinion about what had happened in the ghetto. He used to exchange razor blades for bread while chatting to Pulawski. On one occasion he said that he had not heard from his wife and child in Hamburg for some time; he knew that Hamburg was being bombed by the British and he was worried. Then he pointed to the ruins of the ghetto and added that one must never forget one sad truth: the bombing of Hamburg could never compare with the murder and beastliness that had been perpetrated against innocent people. This sort of remark was rare in Warsaw. It was difficult to find a German who opposed, verbally at any rate, the actions of the Nazis, and that is why I have remembered and recorded this.

The shop became an important part of my life. Friends came to visit me there and I relaxed sufficiently to bring my wife in, though I introduced her as an acquaintance. Pulawski asked very few questions. He knew that some aspects of life were not to be questioned in time of war, but he was, as ever, friendly and courteous. Leaving the shop one day, I bumped into an old student of mine, Wanda Elster, who was a courier for the Jewish Underground Movement. We were both delighted with this chance meeting, and from that time on she brought me a sum of money every month. She would come into the shop and often hand it to Pulawski in a sealed envelope, and he passed it on to me.

On 21st June, 1944, a tragi-comedy was acted out in Pulawski's shop. There were a few friends of his there and we were all invited into a side room where there was a table laden with food and drink. Pulawski seated me at the head of the table, raised a glass of vodka and, wishing me all good fortune, drank. I realised then that the celebration was in my honour, but had no idea what it was all about. I felt rather worried. It turned out that it was my saint's day, since I was called John! None of the guests realised that I was at sea—except Pulawski who, as usual, did not say a word. I hurriedly thanked the guests for helping me to celebrate and it all ended well.

A week later, I was in a chandler's shop at 13, Swietojerska Street at about eleven in the morning. Suddenly I was aware of a scuffle in the street and people running. The Germans were everywhere, and it was rumoured that they had found Jews. I stayed in the shop till it was safe to emerge, and was told that twelve Jews had been hidden at 18, Swietojerska Street, opposite the chandler's shop, two well-known doctors and some children among them. They had been bricked up in one room for over a year and had been looked after by the landlord of the house. They had even had their own telephone and a wireless. The landlord's sister, after an argument with him, had reported their hiding-place to the Gestapo and this, of course, had brought the Germans over hotfoot to arrest them. When one of the Germans poked his head through a tunnel leading to the room, he was immediately shot by one of the occupants. Shooting flared up on both sides; the Germans threw in grenades and all the Jews perished. Two Germans were killed. Looking through the window of the shop, I saw some wounded Germans being taken away in an ambulance and a van removing the personal possessions of the Jews; it was easy to see that they had been very wealthy.

My friendship with Pulawski continued to flourish for some time, but events took a turn which brought it to an end. About two weeks before the Polish Uprising, I said goodbye to him at the end of the day. He went home to Zoliborz and I returned to my shelter in Sapiezynska Street. While we made our farewells, I noticed a stranger looking at me in an odd way. That night was a sleepless one for me. The following morning, when I got to the shop, Pulawski said that he had to confide in me. The man who had looked so strangely at me the previous day had told him that he suspected me of being a Jew. Pulawski had assured the fellow that I was a true Pole; nevertheless, one had to be very careful. The first thing to do was to find out who the stranger was. Pulawski knew his address. I immediately got in touch with a friend of mine who worked for the Polish Underground and he supplied the rest of the details. The man worked for the Germans and was dangerous. As soon as I heard this, I regretfully told Pulawski that our business partnership would have to end as it would be dangerous for me to go on with it. I avoided the neighbourhood, but continued to live in my lodgings in Sapiezynska Street in spite of the danger. I was lucky that this happened so soon before the Polish Uprising, for then the whole situation changed. On the first day of the Uprising, I returned to Ignacy Pulawski's shop, ready to share a common fate with him. The stranger who worked for the Germans was arrested by the Poles and sentenced to death. He was executed among the ruins of the ghetto.

36. A Strange "Purim"

THERE WAS A HOUSE in the town of Piastow, near Warsaw, which was an important landmark in the odyssey of wanderings which my wife and I undertook. The house stood at 37, Sienkiewicz Street and was owned by Mrs. Krzosek-Miaskiewicz. Her daughter, Stefania, was a nun at St. Mary's Convent in Warsaw. My wife was recommended to Mrs. Krzosek-Miaskiewicz when she had to leave her own convent shelter, following the Germans' apprisal of the fact that Jewish children were hidden there. We thought that life in the Krzosek house would be similar to that of the convent; that the same religious atmosphere would prevail and that there would be the same political ties with right-wing underground workers. We were mistaken.

There were a few flats in the house, all occupied by Mrs.

Krzosek's children. These children had been active communists before the war and now worked for the left-wing underground movement. The house was, therefore, a centre of left-wing activities. There were often leading members of the resistance movement in hiding there, and partisans who had to lie low for some time after carrying out a piece of sabotage against German installations. I used to visit my wife there every Sunday, and I always got news of the people who had been there during the week. This was how I learned that the famous poet Stanislaw Jerzy Lec, who was of Jewish extraction, had stayed in the house. They told me that he, with his verve and perfect command of German, had, as an active partisan, taken a group of Poles, all dressed as SS-men, over the heavily guarded Vistula bridge, getting them safely from one forest hideout to another. On another occasion I heard that there was an injured partisan in the house. This was Bolek Alef, who was convalescing at the time.

Mrs. Krzosek-Miaskiewicz had nothing to do with all these activities. Her son and son-in-law arranged all the underground affairs; Mrs. Krzosek merely hid Jews for money. Apart from my wife she hid another woman and two children. Everybody moved freely and fearlessly about the house and garden.

I myself would have been only too delighted to live there, in that active anti-German atmosphere, though all the inhabitants were in constant danger of their lives. But there was no chance of that. They could not risk taking in an unknown Jewish male, since the house was primarily a centre for active resistance workers. Nevertheless, I felt free and happy during the days I spent visiting my wife. I was on friendly terms with all the family and shared my problems and sorrows with them, even taking part in some Catholic festivals which were observed with much devotion. I particularly remember Christmas Eve, 1943, which was very festive.

This happy relationship ended suddenly at the beginning of March 1944. One day, walking down a main thoroughfare of Warsaw, I saw an old Jewish friend from my childhood days, Galewski. He had been with us in the Warsaw ghetto. The street was packed with German officers and we were startled to see each other. Nevertheless, we stopped to talk for a few moments. A brief greeting, and, before an equally brief farewell, my friend said, "Don't forget Purim."* He mentioned the date and disappeared. I never saw him again. At first I did not know what he meant by saying, "Don't forget Purim." How could anyone think of celebrating a Jewish festival? But after a while I understood. It was well known that Hitler often proclaimed in his speeches that the story of Purim, when Haman wanted to exterminate the Jews but was himself killed, would never be repeated. Goebbels in his propaganda messages also used to say that the biblical Feast of Esther was the last one. There would be no more miracles. This, surely, was what my friend had meant. However difficult the situation, one had to go on hoping for a miracle.

The day of Purim arrived and I determined to visit my wife, tell her about meeting my old friend and spend the day with her in honour of the festival, although it was not my usual Sunday visiting day. Apart from the fact that it was Purim, I had influenza and a high temperature and hoped that I could stay overnight in Piastow at Mrs. Krzosek's home. I felt that this would be safer than being ill in my lodgings in Sapiezynska Street.

As was customary, I bought a variety of confectionery and drinks and took them over to Piastow. The young Mrs. Miaskiewicz allowed me to stay for a day or two in her first floor flat. She made up a bed for me while I unpacked my bag of cakes, sweets and drinks. Everyone thought it was my birthday and they prepared to join in the celebration. I told them all to prepare for a party in the evening but assured them that it was nothing to do with a birthday. I wanted to tell them all what we were celebrating and what we were hoping for.

I had been in bed for an hour, to try to get some rest before the evening, when suddenly a neighbour came rushing in to say that the Germans were on the ground floor of the house. The Jewish woman and her two children managed to get into a secret cellar, but my wife and I were trapped. I wanted to jump over the balcony into the garden. This might have saved my wife as, alone,

* Jewish festival commemorating the deliverance of the Jews of the Persian Empire from destruction; the story is told in the Book of Esther.

she could the more easily act the part of a Catholic relative of the family. It was obvious that my presence might mean the end of both of us.

But my plan did not materialise—the Germans were in the room; two big men in leather jackets, with revolvers in their hands. One stayed in the doorway, the other entered and showed his identity card. He was a member of the German Criminal Police (*Kripo*). My wife was sitting with one of the Miaskiewicz children on her lap. The little child of one took one look at the leather-jacketted and jackbooted man and began to cry and shake with fear, clinging tightly to my wife. The man fired questions at me—who I was, what I did and who the woman was who sat there. He disregarded all my replies. I said she was a stranger and that I was not at work because of my influenza. He commanded me to get dressed and said that both of us would be taken to the nearest police station in Pruszkow. I was desperate. My wife said, "We will not go to the police station. We will not be marched through the streets of the town. Whatever is to happen can happen here." Mrs. Miaskiewicz came in at that moment, fell on her knees and appealed to their consciences, begging them not to take us away. To this the German replied furiously, "Hiding Jews in a Polish house to-day! You ought to be shot with them!"

They searched the room thoroughly while we watched and waited, and eventually took a few valuables out of the wardrobe and put them on the table, asking constantly who I was and what I had done before the war. It seemed that they thought I was very rich. This, by the way, was an opinion shared by many—that all Jews were very rich and had large quantities of jewellery. I assured them that I had never been a businessman, had no personal fortune and was prepared to part with what little I had. I took out some things they had overlooked in their search—a gold watch, two rings and 5,000 zlotys in cash. To confirm that I was telling the truth, I showed them my pre-war identity card issued by the Warsaw Municipality, proving that I had been a teacher in various State grammar schools in Warsaw. This was my last hope—and it worked. They scrutinised the card carefully. They took all the things we had and warned Mrs. Miaskiewicz to turn us out at once. It looked as if we were saved. The two men left hurriedly, but we had to leave the house too. Mrs. Miaskiewicz gave us the money to buy our fares to Warsaw.

While this was happening to us, young Mr. Miaskiewicz was sleeping soundly in the room next door, since he was exhausted after endless nights of anti-German sabotage. He woke up as we were preparing to leave the house and was informed of what had happened. He was very angry at having been left out of things and stood, gun in hand, shouting, "I would have shot them. What an opportunity to have missed! Why didn't someone wake me?" How glad we were that nobody had!

A new chapter of journeying started. Maria Rosciszewska, the headmistress, did all she could to find a shelter for my wife. But all the hideouts she could think of were dangerous since they were owned by active underground workers and therefore known and watched by the Gestapo. On one occasion they even had the keys of a flat in which my wife was hiding for a short time. We got through a few desperate weeks, then I decided on a course of action. I got in touch with Mrs. Krzosek-Miaskiewicz at Piastow and asked her if she would agree to take my wife back. It was a dangerous scheme but there was nothing else we could do. She agreed and my wife returned. Our common fate in the months to come was inextricably linked with the house in Piastow.

That Purim of 1944 proved to be a miraculous one.

37. Double Danger

THE POLISH RESISTANCE had been planning, for some weeks, to liquidate the head of the German police in Warsaw. He was well-known for his brutal treatment of Poles, and responsible for many murders. This was General Kutschera, Heinrich Himmler's son-in-law. Members of the underground finally shot him on February 1st, 1944, while he was travelling by car to his headquarters. Reprisals were immediately carried out by the Germans. Hundreds of innocent people were rounded up, imprisoned for a few days and then publicly shot in the streets.

On the day the General was shot I was in the suburb of Mokotow and did not know what was happening in town. Deep in thought, I was strolling at a leisurely pace down the main thoroughfare, oblivious of the fact that the street was practically empty, though it was usually busy and packed with people. It was the time when street loudspeakers usually broadcast the news bulletins from the various front lines. Generally hundreds of people stopped to listen but now I found myself alone. I listened carefully, barely aware that there was no one else listening with me. Suddenly, an open van drove past. There were men sitting in a double row at the back, their hands above their heads. Standing between the two rows were SS-men, machine-guns pointing and at the ready. I was terrified and rooted to the spot. I had no idea what had happened. The SS smiled at me and I smiled back but I sensed danger. The van passed and I heard a voice calling out from behind a gate, "Lunatic! How can you just stand there when people are being rounded up to be shot!" I had been lucky. The number of people arrested had been large enough to satisfy the Germans. Possibly the Germans thought I was a member of the secret police, otherwise I would surely not have been standing there so confidently and returning their smiles. Who knows how many Jews, posing as Poles, were killed as a result of the General's assassination?

Another incident. It was very dark outside but there was still an hour to curfew. I was on my way to my lodgings in Sapiezynska Street and wondered how to spend this last hour since I never went indoors till I really had to. I happened to be in front of the Capuchin Church in Miodowa Street. It was open, so I went in. The interior was silent as the grave. A tiny lamp was burning, faintly illuminating the statue of the Virgin and Child. I could just discern a few scattered worshippers, mainly old women, mumbling a last few words before returning home. I sat alone in a pew, deep in thought. The vanished world stood before me and I saw all my relatives and friends vividly. They were followed by clear images of my colleagues and hundreds of pupils, who had all perished in the past year. If it were not for the all-pervading smell of incense, it would have been easy to forget that I was in a church. A voice tore across my reverie, "What are you doing here?" It was a sacristan. "What do you want?" I replied, "I have come to say the last Pater Noster. This is on my way home and I come in every night." "Nonsense," he said, "I know your sort! You want to use the church as a cover for your political activities. Get out at once!" I felt better. I saw that he did not take me for a Jew. "What are you talking about?" The sacristan pulled out an illegal news sheet printed by the underground and said, "You see, leaflets like these are slipped into all the missals sometime during the evening. That is probably your work!" It was natural that he should suspect me, as generally there was no sign of young people at evening prayers, and here was I, sitting amongst the old women! I assured him that I had nothing to do with any illegal printing, but snatched the pamphlet and ran off home. From it I learned of the defeats that the Germans had sustained in all theatres of war. It was a great comfort to me.

In Warsaw, travelling by bus was hazardous. The Germans often stopped buses, ordered the passengers off and searched them thoroughly. All Poles had to show their identity cards and written evidence of address and job. This was to ascertain whether they were helping the war effort on behalf of the Germans. This type of sudden search always produced casualties, so I avoided the town buses as much as possible and walked whenever I could, whatever the distance. Other Jews in hiding behaved in the same way.

One day I took a chance and caught a bus. It was crowded and we were packed tightly together. In the crush, I noticed an acquaintance sitting in a corner seat. He was a very cultivated man, a well-known pre-war socialist from Krakow who now went under the name of Kaminski. From our first meeting some months before, I had suspected that he was of Jewish origin. Doubtless he had the same suspicion about me but we did not discuss this delicate matter. In conversation, however, he often mentioned the names of well-known Jewish socialists and asked if I had known them. He nevertheless acted the part of a Pole extremely well. His bearing and appearance, his use of language and accent successfully demonstrated that he had no Jewish connections. One thing could be divined—he was an active and capable underground worker.

When Mr. Kaminski saw me in the bus I sensed his sudden nervousness. Something troubled him about my presence; he seemed to be visibly collapsing. We were some distance from each other. We glanced briefly at each other and said nothing. Suddenly I saw Germans through the window. They signalled for the bus to halt, poured in onto the platform and ordered all passengers to move up inside. They signalled again and the bus moved on, complete with its new load of passengers. Silence fell on us all. It was obvious everybody was under arrest; they were only driving on till they could get to a convenient place where we could be searched. I stole a glance at Mr. Kaminski's waxen face. In those few moments he seemed to have aged by half a century. The Germans scrutinised all the passengers, smiling and pleased to see us all in terror for our lives. In a short while they again ordered the bus to halt, and simply got off. On this one occasion they were just using public transport to get from one part of town to another. All the passengers breathed freely again. Mr. Kaminski and I got off at the next stop. I told him that he seemed to have lost his head. "What about you?" he said, "do you know what you looked like?" "Me?" I said, "Well, I have good reason." "And what about me?" Kaminski hissed back, "am I a Greek or a Turk?" He added that he was carrying some very valuable documents.

A further illustration of life on the Aryan side. There was a chandler's shop at 6, Franciscan Street. I often went in and regarded the proprietor as a very decent fellow. Every morning I would stop there, have a chat and move on. One day during the winter of 1944 I was in the shop having my talk when two SS men came in, guns in hand. They yelled out an order, "Hands up!" This meant me, not the proprietor, with whom they seemed rather friendly. They told him that a bomb had been thrown not far from the shop and they had to find the culprit. I stayed calm and said pleasantly to the shopkeeper, "We will finish our chat later. I'll come in after lunch." One of the Germans reared up at me, shouting, "Spy! You are a spy!" The shopkeeper reassured him, saying I was trustworthy and not in any way connected with subversive activities. The Germans calmed down and I got out of the shop alive. I wondered why the Germans had listened so readily to the shopkeeper but I found out soon enough. During the first day of the Polish Uprising he was arrested by the Polish authorities, court-martialled and shot as a collaborator and informer. No wonder the Germans had believed him when he testified to my good character!

Another curious incident. The Old City of Warsaw was filled with narrow streets and tiny ancient houses. At that time hostages were being rounded up as a reprisal for various acts of sabotage. I went out of a little shop into Piwna Street to find it completely deserted. A detachment of six Germans appeared, walking abreast and taking up the whole width of the street, and all armed with guns. Backing into the shop was out of the question. I had to stand my ground in spite of the danger. There were two courses of action open to me; either walking off briskly down a side turning, which on reflection seemed foolish, as they would be sure to give chase or to shoot; or walking straight on to meet them. I decided on the second course. I approached them with a firm step, mumbled an excuse me, and pushed my way through them. It worked. I walked on and saw an old woman devoutly crossing herself. She called out to me, "What luck you had! What luck you had!"

These were the kind of dangers one had to face even when Jews were fully accepted as Poles. This hazard was at its worst at the time of the Polish Uprising in the summer of 1944. I witnessed one incident in the Old City. One of my former students was a courier for the Polish fighters. Heedless of danger, she fearlessly carried military despatches from one fighting group to another. Until the last moment she was accepted as a Catholic. She fell fighting and I attended the funeral. She was buried in haste in the courtyard of 13, Franciscan Street; a priest said a few brief prayers and an officer praised the heroism of the youth of Poland but no one, except me, knew that she was a Jewish girl who had escaped from the ghetto. Many Jews died in this way; having survived the first hazard of being Jews, they perished as Poles.

38. Passion Week, Warsaw 1944

PASSION WEEK was always observed with great devotion in Poland. It is the week before Easter and commemorates the events leading to the crucifixion of Jesus. Jews also had cause to remember Passion Week, since during that time hatred against them reached a pitch unknown during the rest of the year.

It was Passion Week, 1944, and officially Warsaw had no Jews. The churches were packed from morning till night. Men, women and children found religion a great source of inspiration and comfort and often stayed for private prayer long after the services had ended. In this sort of bustle, a hidden Jew felt safer than in the calm of normal days in the church, though the atmosphere of approaching Easter was oppressive. The Cathedral of St. John in the Old City was very large and always full, and the odd Jew could easily escape detection. It was disturbing, however, during the actual service, to listen to the sermons which were, as always, unchanged in attitude and content, in spite of the cataclysm which had fallen on us.

I particularly remember one Mass in the Jesuit Church near the Cathedral. The church was overcrowded and among the congregation was at least one Jew in hiding. The Mass proceeded and then a priest ascended the pulpit. I noticed that he put on a skullcap before delivering his sermon; I had not seen this done in other Catholic churches. His theme was the trial of Jesus and his death.

He portrayed vividly the agony on the cross, and took the opportunity of attacking the Pharisees, constantly referring to them as Jews and speaking with marked venom. From the time that Ignatius Loyola founded the Society of Jesus in the sixteenth century, it has displayed signs of antisemitism. Nevertheless, even the most antisemitic of Jesuits could not have visualised the bloodbath in the capital city of Poland. The priest spoke, of course, of the Jews of Roman times, but the twist of his argument was such that he could easily have been referring to modern Jewry. The worshippers, the majority of them ordinary artisans living in the Old City, listened in silence. For them Jews were Jews, those of old being equated with those of the present day. They were all responsible for the death of Jesus, and were all enemies of Christianity.

This sort of service, repeated daily in Passion Week, inevitably led us, as Jews in hiding, to speculate about the root causes of such attitudes. The worst atrocities against us had been perpetrated by our common enemy in a country whose population consisted of devout Catholics. To what extent was the church, through its modes of teaching, responsible for what happened?

These effects of ecclesiastical indoctrination were seen with the greatest clarity on Good Friday. The Good Friday of 1944 was, for me, one of the most difficult days on the Aryan side. It started normally enough, with a visit to one of the churches in the Old City. I was turning the pages of a missal. I read the message of Easter, the story of Jesus being handed over to the Romans. The priests in Jerusalem delivered him to Pontius Pilate so that he could pass sentence. Pilate begged the Jews to agree to his release. He thought that the "king of the Jews" was innocent. The priests were obstinate and demanded that he be crucified; they told Pilate that they were loyal to Rome and her Emperor, and that whoever freed Jesus would be guilty of treason.

I read also the mediaeval hymns (the collection called *Gorzkie Zale*) bewailing the fate of Jesus and noted how, in their scornful words, all Jews were blamed and condemned. It is hard to accuse the masses who are poisoned by such doctrines. One thinks now with great respect of those thousands of Poles who, notwithstanding the feeling around Passion Week, risked their lives frequently to rescue the few Jews who were left.

I left the church. It was a bright and sunny day but I could not rid myself of the thoughts which had obsessed me in the church. I had a few things to attend to, such as collecting some money owing to me for my sugar sales. I also had to visit a lawyer, Gozdziewski, in Kredytowa Street, who had promised to make out a new identity card for my wife. Her original one had been stolen a few days before. On my way to the lawyer I had to walk down Marszalkowska Street, which was very crowded. The shops were packed with people buying food for the Easter holiday. I was mingling with the crowds, certain that no one would notice me. Suddenly I was aware that I was not alone; I was being followed by a stranger. I began to hurry, but pretended not to notice that I was being tailed. At my destination, 16, Kredytowa Street, I saw that the stranger had stopped at the gate with me. I heard one word, "Stop!" I sized him up and wondered what he wanted and who he was. He showed me his badge—he was a member of the Criminal Police—and the well-known interrogation started. He asked for my identity card and shot a series of questions at me about address, relatives and job. I had a prepared reply to each question and at that moment all seemed well. Two Polish policemen materialised from nowhere and he asked them to wait as he wanted them to take an arrested man to the police station. The situation seemed grave. I pretended ignorance—and the word Jew had not, so far, been mentioned. When I protested sharply, he grabbed his revolver. "We'll teach you Jewish spies!" He hit me in the face; he had obviously divined the truth. I went on hoping for a miracle. All that was left was bribery. I said, "I have just collected a lot of money. Take it and let me go." "How much?" he asked. "I don't know—you can have it all." He liked this reply. I took out a roll of banknotes and said again, "This is all I have." He was pleased with the size of the roll though he did not stop to count it. "I like Jews like you," he said, "generally Jews bargain. Your attitude is not Jewish at all." One thing had annoyed him, however. I should have admitted being a Jew straight away and the situation would never have arisen. He asked me to wait while he dealt with the two policemen who were still waiting to take me away.

His attitude suddenly changed and he became very friendly; he was even prepared to give me his telephone number. I could ring him whenever I was in trouble. I thanked him profusely, but asked him one question. How was it possible to pick out one suspect in a teeming, crowded street? The reply was simple. "First of all, shave off your Polish-type moustache! All Jews in hiding try to pass as Poles and think that a moustache is the answer. That is ridiculous. Secondly, you should clean your shoes every day. You can always recognise Jews by their filthy shoes. Particularly in streets like Marszalkowska and Kredytowa." I thanked him for these tips and departed. I stayed as long as I could in the lawyer's flat, as I was still afraid that someone might be waiting for me in the street.

When I returned to my business partner, Ignacy Pulawski, I had to say that I had had an accident and could not give him the money I owed him, which amounted to 50,000 zlotys. Pulawski asked no questions. He probably realised what had happened. I went on working and repaid my debt to him in weekly instalments. I was lucky to have some financial help from Mrs. Maria Rosciszewska and Wanda Elster.

I went on paying until the Polish Uprising.

39. The "New Order" Crumbles

FOR WEEKS before the Polish Uprising on 1st August, 1944, the atmosphere in Warsaw was electric. Everyone sensed, in various ways, the signs of impending liberation. The hidden Jews waited —with mixed feelings. We were both sad and happy. Sad, because each of us carried in his heart the sufferings of the vanished millions who had not survived to see the defeat of our greatest enemy; happy, because we felt that this was the end of the years of war and tragedy, and that in a matter of days the reign of terror would be over.

The days before the Uprising rang with the news from the Eastern front. The sounds of gunfire were, for us, a veritable symphony, playing tunes of freedom. We listened day and night as the sounds moved closer. As they grew louder, our hopes soared higher. Five years of waiting for these noisy, sleepless nights! News came daily of parts of Poland that had been liberated. News from Lublin and Bialystok; and the Soviet armies were coming to Otwock—a short step from Warsaw. Most important, the Jews in Warsaw were certain that Majdanek, Belzec, Sobibor and Treblinka, the extermination camps in the East, were at last in Soviet hands.

There were other signs of the defeat of Germany. All day remnants of the broken German army straggled through the streets of Warsaw. They were tired, dirty and hungry deserters. These representatives of the erstwhile *Herrenvolk* now looked like the Jewish victims they had hounded out of the cities of Europe to their death. Thousands of people stood all day to watch the beggarly procession of soldiers. The atmosphere was relaxed. No one was afraid any more. The Poles openly made cheap jokes about the former murderers and rulers of Europe.

Among the thousands of observers were a few Jews who could not stare hard enough at the spectacle. Watching the retreating army move from East to West reminded one of former days. One remembered the weeks before the outbreak of war between Russia and Germany in June 1941. Then, one saw the German armies moving from West to East, preparing to attack and certain of a speedy victory. In 1941, they marched through the ghetto streets at night, when the town was deserted. They marched through Wola, Chlodna Street, Elektoralna and Senatorska and crossed the Vistula bridge, getting nearer and nearer to the Soviet frontier. Jews stood all night in darkened rooms looking through cracks in the shutters to see the varied units and their equipment. We were certain that war with Russia spelled freedom overnight. I was standing with Janusz Korczak at the windows of 33, Chlodna Street. We stared from the orphanage at the massed army, and noted the enormous tanks. Written on them was "Stalin, *wir kommen*—We're coming, Stalin!" Dr. Korczak thought this was a happy omen for the Jews. He was so certain that in a matter of days Russia would crush the Germans. It was a ray of hope for every Jew behind the ghetto walls.

The dream lasted for over three years, and a sea of blood and tears drowned millions of Jews. Now the few survivors watched for hours on end as the former heroes dragged wearily back to Germany, themselves the victims of war.

With the beaten Germans came their families. The plump wives were clutching stolen property to take home with them. Hundreds of vans were packed tightly with furniture, bedding and other household effects. Everything was being rushed away to prevent its falling into Soviet hands. The German civil servants, Gestapo and police were scuttling out like rats from a sinking ship. They were terror-stricken, remembering all they had done in the city, and knowing they would be called to account for looting and cold-blooded murder.

Suddenly, posters appeared on the hoardings: all men between twelve and sixty were to report for work. They were to dig trenches and build fortifications to save Europe from Jews and communists. We were all rather worried. What now? Of course, no one would volunteer for this kind of job. I waited to see how the Poles would respond to this "patriotic" call. I did not have long to wait. In the Old City, eleven people reported for work, and these, by popular opinion, were thought slightly mad.

Generally speaking, Jews were not mentioned at this time. They might never have existed; people were occupied with more important matters. Wherever possible, German arsenals and stores were raided to build up stocks of arms and goods. The glorious summer days of July were spent dragging sacks and barrels through the streets. Any available container was packed to capacity with goods, food and whatever there was for the taking. In haste, things were dropped, and the streets of the Old City had a trail of dyestuffs along the pavements. Red, green, blue and yellow mixed in unforgettable patterns in an otherwise dull street.

It was all festive and joyful and the streets were jammed with noisy crowds. The Jews, however, were overcome with other emotions. Without doubt we had waited for years for this moment, the end of the "New Order". It was coming fast, but sadness was ever present. Each hidden Jew asked himself: Is this German defeat the beginning of the punishment they so richly deserve for their crimes? Can there ever be sufficient punishment?

I remembered the story of the flood, when all humanity was brought to book. Surely a nation who could produce so many murderers had earned divine retribution of floodlike dimensions.

It is not surprising that, when everybody was so happy, the Jews remained unaffected by what was happening around them.

The Polish Uprising brought a new disaster to the few surviving Jews.

40. The Battle Begins

PEOPLE IN THE STREETS were inspired by the news from the front line; everyone thought that the liberation of Warsaw was at hand. The gunfire from the front sounded as loud as if it were right in the town. We waited, counting the hours and the minutes.

About the actual Uprising, planned against the Germans—not a word. The secret was well kept and plans were passed by word of mouth to a few trusty group leaders. Little of the information penetrated through to the few hidden Jews. Yet in the meantime one still had to attend to the business of hiding and staying alive. My wife was still at Piastow, near Warsaw. I was in Warsaw, changing my hiding place every day, though my official permanent residence was still at Sapiezynska Street. The night before the Uprising I decided to stay with a friend in the Mokotow district. He owned a flat and was a professional soldier. He was under suspicion himself as he had a Jewish wife, whom he had kept hidden in the country with his parents throughout the war. During the day he worked in the Resistance movement in Warsaw, and returned to his wife every evening. We had known each other well long before the war and he was a great help to me at this time. Before going off at night he always gave me the key to his flat, so I was invariably provided with an emergency hiding-place.

Curfew was approaching. Looking out of the window of the Mokotow flat, I saw the street growing quieter and emptier. The noise of gunfire seemed nearer and louder. The street was intensely dark when Soviet planes appeared overhead, dropping flares onto the city. In seconds, the city was lit up, as if by hundreds of gleaming chandeliers; flares hung suspended in the air. I looked, and thought of the countless candelabra that had burned so brightly in the synagogues of hundreds of Jewish towns.

Suddenly, I heard a knocking at the door, and on the threshold stood an officer of the Polish police. He was a neighbour of mine and lived in another room in the same flat. He greeted me courteously but seemed very agitated. He started the conversation by talking about the Russians and said he was sure that in a day or two Warsaw would be free; but he hoped that the new régime would not accuse him too harshly. Being in the Polish police, which was recognised by the Germans, he had nevertheless always tried to defend Polish interests. I felt that all this was just a preamble. He continued to speak about his actions as a policeman and tried to show me that he had been completely loyal to Poland. For example, he said that he had known that my wife and I had hidden in the flat from time to time only because we were Jews, but had said nothing. Now he hoped that in the days to come, if he should be brought to justice, we would defend him. It would have been foolish to engage him in a discussion about my Jewishness, so, in a friendly manner, I tried to calm him down and said decent people had nothing to worry about. He would surely not be accused. He insisted that I have tea with him and his wife. I went, thinking it wiser, since I still had to spend a night under the same roof as the man and he could easily have gone out and reported my presence.

In the morning, on August 1st, 1944, I decided to go back to the Old City. I walked there and it took me about two hours. Tension was high among the Poles and among the Germans, but still not a word about the Uprising. By nine o'clock I had arrived in the Old City. I had no personal contacts and wondered how to spend the long, bright day. Wearily I urged the hours along, meandering among the brisk, expectant crowds. As yet, I had no inkling of what was going to happen. Lunchtime approached. I decided to go to the restaurant in St. Joseph's Community Centre in Severynow Street; perhaps I might glean a few facts there. I went into the restaurant—to find it completely empty. The tables were set, the doors open, but there was no sign of life. A nun glided in and, with a frightened expression, looked hard at me.

She seemed to be pitying me. She asked if I knew what was happening outside; the Uprising was due to start in two hours. It was three o'clock and I was the only person who had lunch there, as quietly as ever before. It was the last cooked meal I was to have for the next eight weeks.

I stepped out to find Krakowskie Przedmiescie Street in a turmoil. Crowds were milling around, all on the run. German police and soldiers were lined up in front of the government buildings, guns in hands. I did not hurry; I simply wondered where to go. Perhaps the best thing would be to go back to Mokotow and stay with my Polish police neighbour. He was afraid and so was I. We had that in common, at least.

I got as far as Krolewska Street but could get no further. I was in the front line and there was shooting on all sides. German soldiers were lying on the pavements, firing up at buildings that had been taken over by the Polish fighters. All the houses and shops were tightly shuttered and I just stood there with nowhere to hide. To walk on to Mokotow was out of the question. I had to try to get back to the Old City. There at least I had an old friend, Ignacy Pulawski. Now I could return to him without being afraid of informers.

Bent double, I ran through Pilsudzki Square, rechristened Hitler Square. It was lined with armed Germans. Apart from myself there was no other civilian to be seen. The Germans smiled at my distress. In Senatorska Street, hard by Dr. Fischer's residence, a motor bicycle drew up with two Germans. Suddenly, Poles appeared in all doorways and hurled grenades. The cycle and the two Germans were blown to pieces. It was about five o'clock, zero hour according to my informant in the restaurant. I got to Nowiniarska Street, and saw columns of German cars driving along by the walls of the Warsaw ghetto. They were being shot at from various side streets but offered no return-fire.

At the corner of Franciscan and Nowiniarska Streets, I saw a small hunchback holding a sub-machine gun and firing steadily at the German file of cars. The bullets bounded off the ghetto walls. When he saw me, he held out the machine gun and said, "Citizen, you fire a salvo. It is high time you had a go." I wondered what he meant; did he really know who I was? I gladly fired a round of bullets, however. I felt that I had been accorded the greatest honour possible.

Standing in front of Pulawski's shop at 18, Nowiniarska Street, I saw a young man of about twenty in civilian clothes with the Polish national emblem, an eagle, on his hat. He held a revolver. He stopped beside me and said, saluting, "Sir, the arsenal is at your disposal." At first I was bewildered, but quickly realised that he thought I was Pulawski. The shop next door sold stationery but I had noted that it was open only one day in three. Pulawski had told me confidentially that in the cellar below the stationer's there was a secret arsenal. Now I understood. The young man was in a hurry to join his unit, and so was handing it over, to Pulawski as he thought. I smiled and took over the arsenal. Joyfully I went into Pulawski's office and told him the news. All was gay and happy at Pulawski's, as if it were all over. A group of Polish friends were toasting the day's events in vodka. I thought the rejoicing was premature but was afraid of showing my fears, and said nothing of what I had seen and done in the last few hours.

Pulawski welcomed me with open arms. He was delighted to see me and have me with him. We stayed together for a month, and I relived some experiences that reminded me vividly of my last days in the ghetto.

After the first night there, everyone quickly realised that the end was still a long way off. A German tank came down the street, stopped at the corner of Franciscan and Nowiniarska Streets, and proceeded to fire at all the houses. The bombardment was fierce and marked the beginning of a new battle that was to continue for over two months.

41. Jewish Fighters in the Old City

THE EARLY DAYS of the Polish Uprising in the Old City were filled with joy and hope. The streets were crowded. Polish national flags, draped over balconies and hanging out of windows, spread the glad tidings of a freedom that was here to stay. All the churches of the Old City were packed with worshippers attending special thanksgiving services.

Among the thousands in the streets one could see, here and there, a few Jews. They were mainly young men and women, with just a few older people, out at last from their hiding places, and breathing freely for the first time in four years. Some of the Jews were old friends of mine and our joy at meeting was indescribable. But we still asked; "Is this really the end of the war? Has the Uprising overpowered the Germans? Are we really free?" Their years of tragedy had left their mark on all the Jews. Their eyes were still filled with the terror of what had been.

The Old City was completely cut off from the rest of the town. Gunfire could be heard coming from other quarters, but it did not affect the peace and calm that reigned here. Nevertheless, people were being asked to come and build barricades in the streets. A temporary barricade of tables and chairs was hastily erected at the corner of Franciscan and Nowiniarska Streets, immediately opposite the ghetto wall. People hurried over with furniture, pieces of wood and packing cases and in a short while the makeshift rampart was three feet high. Jews flung themselves into this sacred work with all their remaining energy. Many, however, regarded it as foolish in the light of their previous knowledge of German strength. No improvised, flimsy structure could withstand a mechanised onslaught. However, the work proceeded.

Thousands of people evacuating other parts of the city were crowding into the old section. They had a lot to tell of German cruelty and of the murderous behaviour of General Vlasov's unit, a group of Soviet prisoners-of-war turned collaborators. People fled, leaving their houses, shops and possessions behind, seeking safety in the Old City, for that, in those early days, really seemed to be the quietest place. A large group of men, women and children came from Senatorska Street. They had been hiding for two days in the crypt of St. Anthony's, and described their fearful experiences after the Germans had taken over the street and the church. The Poles were divided into two groups. One group was sent to the German-occupied part of the city while the other was told to run to the "Polish bandits" in the Old City. To the Germans it was all a huge joke. They would get them all in the end anyhow. They machine-gunned those running towards the Old City and many fell dead, among them the famous priest Stanislaw Trzeciak. The few Jews who listened to this tale could have added many more facts about the activities of this priest, who was killed, ironically, by a German bullet. He had inflamed and poisoned the minds of the Polish masses by his reactionary speeches and writings, was also an active contributor to the Nazi press, his sole topic being anti-Jewish propaganda. But this was not the time to tell these tales. Silence was still imperative.

Peace and calm in the Old City were short lived. There was a sudden frontal attack. The streets were bombarded from all sides and houses collapsed in ruins. Fires were raging everywhere and the death toll rose every hour. For the Jews, inactivity was out of the question. The Poles were coming to grips with the arch-enemy, and our duty as citizens and fellow sufferers was to assist them. Hundreds joined in the battles, and died as heroes; but they fought and died as Poles, since they still kept their acquired names and their Jewish origin was usually unsuspected. I, too, had decided to keep my name of Jan Zielinski throughout the Uprising and to stay with my Polish friends. On the first day of battle I joined a Civil Defence Committee and had many dangerous tasks to perform.

The whole of the civilian population was now living in cellars and among ruins; it was dangerous to wander about the street. Bombs and grenades were exploding everywhere. I lived in a cellar at 13, Franciscan Street with Ignacy Pulawksi and a group of his friends. We read about the Jewish Fighting Unit in a Polish newspaper; it was active in the Old City and called on all surviving Jews to join in the fight against the enemy. Some of those who read this burst out laughing. The idea of Jews fighting! The idea of Jews helping to save Poland! They found it ludicrous. Even the initials of the organisation amused them—JOB. Ignacy Pulawski was furious with them. When I met some of the members of the Jewish Fighting Unit, survivors of the Ghetto Uprising, who now marched, gun in hand, through the Old City, I was greatly moved. I asked myself: were they not brave enough in the ghetto a year ago; was it not a fact that they were the very personification of heroism? Was it necessary for them to demonstrate their valour yet again?

At this time my main job was to carry the wounded from Franciscan Street to the Military Hospital in Dluga Street. This task was carried out all day and night under a hail of bullets. The porter at 13, Franciscan Street was in charge of Civil Defence for the street, but he showed little patriotism. He cared neither for his fellow-men nor for his country. He would not sit in the cellar but stayed in his flat with friends, drinking incessantly. They sang at the tops of their voices the famous song of the fighters, "When a Soldier Carries his Heart in His Kit-bag. . . ."

But the porter remembered me. When there was a particularly unpleasant job to do he would yell for me to come up from the cellar. All my cellar friends remarked on this, but I alone knew that he was picking on the hidden Jew. At the most dangerous moments, when grenades were exploding all round the house, this "patriot" would call me up to bury the dead in the court-yard. People asked, "Why now? Surely the corpses can wait till it's a bit less dangerous." It made no difference; an order was an order. Bent double, I and one other person would go out and bury four or five of the dead. While we were digging the grave we would be violently shaken by shrapnel and explosions. In the distance we would hear the drunken singing of the porter and his friends. The grave was dug in haste and fear—and deeply. The deeper the grave, the safer we were. When the grave was ready, my companion would say, "The dead can wait. Let's stay in this trench till it gets quieter." He was right, of course, and we stayed there for some time. We buried the dead when the firing temporarily ceased.

Ignacy Pulawski understood what was happening, and was furious. On one occasion, when we heard that famous yell, "Mr. Zielinski!" yet again, Pulawski jumped up and said he would go instead. The task was to carry wounded to hospital. He left, and returned some hours later with his head heavily bandaged; he had been wounded while carrying a patient and was lucky to have survived.

The heroism of the Polish fighters cannot be adequately described. Each house was defended and fought over. Inch by inch the fighters retreated and inch by inch the Germans won back street after street.

I was fortunate that my friend Jan Piechowicz, the pre-war civil servant, had not forgotten me. He was in the Old City and became one of its greatest heroes; his exploits were legend. He would come every day, under fire, with his coat collar turned up, and inquire after me. The neighbours in the cellar treated me with deference because of these daily visits. That this great man should come so often at the risk of his own life was, to them, remarkable. Piechowicz often whispered in my ear, "I come as often as this because I don't want them to suspect that you're a Jew."

Among those who sat in the cellar at number 13 was a Chinese. During the whole of the Uprising he shook with terror. He lay wrapped in blankets, shivering, his head covered to deaden the sound of the gunfire. Piechowicz always looked down at him and laughed. This amused us all.

The cellar became more and more crowded with people from other houses. The upper floors of number 13 had disappeared now. All that was left was the basement and the ground floor. Thousands of people passed through and walked from street to street through a labyrinth of cellars, all connected by means of holes cut in the masonry. In this mass of people, I once noticed a relative of mine, Rachel Upfal from Warsaw. We glanced briefly at each other, but we neither approached each other nor spoke. The climate was still anti-Jewish and this aspect worsened as the Uprising collapsed. The Jews were again in a hopeless position. For them there was no way out. It was obvious that the Germans would re-occupy the city, and any Jew discovered there was a dead man. The nearer the end of the battle, the greater the problem among the blazing debris. In this way many Jews who had survived the horrors of the ghetto and of hiding on the Aryan side had again to live through a similar nightmare, but this time completely isolated, relying on their own initiative for survival.

How many Jews actually died in the Polish Uprising will never be known.

42. The Jews from Auschwitz (August, 1944)

IT WAS SUNDAY MORNING, the sixth day of the Polish Uprising. The Old City was alive with the news that the ruins of the ghetto and the *Umschlagplatz* had been liberated. Everyone was talking about the fierce battles that had taken place during the night. The Polish fighters had mounted a surprise attack and liberated the imported Jewish slave workers.

Hundreds of people were assembling at the corner of Franciscan and Nowiniarska Streets, staring at a strange tableau. A few dozen men were tearing down the old provisional barricade and building another. The new one had a much firmer structure, to make it proof against tanks and armoured cars. It was easy to see that the men were newly released from a prison camp; they wore striped suits and small striped hats and their general appearance was frightful. They worked with diligence, watched over by four young armed men, guns at the ready. The crowd kept shouting questions at the workers, but got no reply as they did not understand a word of Polish. I asked one of the Polish guards what was happening and who these workers were. He answered briskly, "These are Jews whom we took as prisoners during the night. They come from abroad and don't know any Polish." I was horrified to hear this reply. The Jews had not been liberated, but had been taken prisoner. This turned out to be a misunderstanding.

I heard that the HQ of the officer in charge of the young Poles was at 12, Franciscan Street. I went to see him, without revealing my exact identity, and after my intervention the Jews were freed and the young armed guards disappeared. A few hours later the Jews appeared in better clothing. They were also given food, and their morale was so much higher that no one seeing them in the street could guess where they had come from nor what horrors they had lived through. They returned willingly to the job of building the barricade near the ghetto wall. There were some capable engineers and professional builders among them. Their finished job, in contrast to all the other rickety structures that had been thrown together, was made of steel and iron; and in the ensuing four-week battle, it protected the streets of the Old City and saved hundreds from certain death.

In general, the attitude of the Poles to the foreign Jews during that month was exemplary. The Jews themselves confirmed this.

From the moment of the liberation, the foreign Jews had sought contact with the hidden Jews of the Old City. Undoubtedly, the easiest way to achieve this would have been through the Jewish Fighting Unit. Anyhow, all the Jews in the Old City were themselves most anxious to make contact. We all wanted to know where they had been, what they had gone through, where they came from, how they got to Poland and, above all, what sort of work they had done in the ghetto ruins.

The foreigners threw themselves into the Old City battle with great energy. They fought side by side with the Poles and showed real heroism in the defence of the historical part of the city. More than once, I had to bury one of them. One, an officer, fell while leading his unit to the battle area. He was a Hungarian Jew, and some of his friends and two Polish officers attended his hurried funeral. When we had completed the burial, one of the friends moved to one side and expressed his farewell with the traditional Kaddish.* The officers saluted and the sound of gunfire accompanied the only Hebrew prayer ever said for a fallen fighter at this time.

From time to time, I was able to have a brief chat with one of the newcomers. It was easier to talk to them in German, but this would have been dangerous during the days of fighting, when the very sound of German was enough to have one accused of espionage.

One of them, a well-known surgeon from Budapest, told me a great deal. During the fighting in the Old City, he was senior surgeon in the Dluga Street Military Hospital. He worked day and

* A prayer for the Jewish mourner.

night and performed hundreds of operations. He was very modest, but was devoted to his profession and saved many lives, which enhanced his reputation as an outstanding character as well as a great doctor. He was my neighbour at night in the cellar at 13, Franciscan Street, and he told me then that his companions had been brought to Warsaw directly from Auschwitz. They were from France, Greece, Czechoslovakia, Hungary and elsewhere. At the beginning they had worked with Poles at clearing the ghetto debris. Executions were often carried out among the ruins, of Poles as well as Jews. The Jews who were shot were mainly those who had been caught on the Aryan side in Warsaw and taken there for killing. To leave as little trace as possible of these mass murders, a crematorium had been built and all the bodies were burnt. The cremation was one of the jobs of the foreign Jews.

The doctor also told me some interesting details about the ruins themselves. Large parties of Polish workers came in every day for work and were very diligent in searching for the fortunes of the Jews, which they expected to find concealed there. They often found, hidden away in cellars, charred bodies dating back to the time of the Ghetto Uprising, but they also found money and jewellery on occasion. In the spring of 1944, a whole year after that Uprising, two Jews, barely alive, were dragged out of the ruins. They had managed to hide the whole time. Of course, they were immediately shot by the Germans.

As the gunfire from the eastern front grew louder, the majority of the foreign Jews working in the ruins of the ghetto were sent to Germany, but no one ever found out what happened to them. Those who, surprisingly, were retained in the ghetto by the Germans, were miraculously freed by the Poles. The doctor, who fell into this category, was certain that if the Poles had not intervened they would have been shot. He himself could not understand the deportations to Germany; they all expected to be shot together in the ghetto.

It was tragic to listen to his tales of the fate of the Hungarian Jews in Auschwitz. He had lost all his relatives there. None of the Hungarian Jews had been aware of what had previously happened in Poland and so had never expected the fate that overtook them.

They had been led to believe that they were being sent to labour camps.

The situation for the foreign Jews became perilous when the civilian population finally had to evacuate the Old City, by order of the Germans. They were in a hopeless position; not knowing the language or having any friends, there was no escape route for them. The Poles had surrendered the Old City and departed; the military units had escaped through the sewers and were joining the resistance groups in order to fight again. Possibly the foreigners were also allowed to escape via the sewers. I saw a few of them in the town when I had managed to escape. When I asked them about their companions they knew nothing at all. I never found out what happened to the surgeon.

43. The Ruins

EVEN AFTER APRIL, 1943, the ghetto walls still stood as a barrier and dividing line between that area and the rest of the town, though until August of the following year we were able to witness a great deal that happened in the ruins. We could, however, only watch from afar, as every sign of habitation was carefully erased. But the outer wall of the "valley of death" was left untouched. The entrance to the ghetto was kept locked as before, thus prohibiting entry by any member of the general population.

It was not surprising, then, that as soon as the Poles had liberated the Jewish workers and entry was easy, any surviving Jew would want to see with his own eyes what was left of a life that had been so dear to him. But to make a pilgrimage alone to this holy spot was hard to contemplate. One had neither the courage nor the emotional strength. The silence and the emptiness that enveloped those ruins filled one with dread and awe. Any Jew who had lived in the ghetto till the Uprising of 1943 had known the streets and alleys filled with life and movement and, in spite of everything, hope. They were now an unimaginable wilderness. So, after many deliberations, I decided to ask my landlord, Jan Witkowski, to accompany me on a visit there. I made the request with tact and diplomacy. The idea appealed to him. He hoped to find old Jewish fortunes hidden away. His needs and demands were modest; he would have been content to find some old clothes, old shoes, crockery, cutlery and perhaps some firewood.

We both set out on this sad adventure the day after the ghetto was liberated. Above all, I wanted to see all the places and buildings that would remind me of former years. I wanted to see my own home, the schools where I had taught and all the buildings that were in any way connected with friends and relatives. We entered the ghetto through Krasinski Square and started walking over the uneven roads till we reached Zamenhof Street. The palpable silence, the stark ruins, made even my companion shudder. We did not see a single soul. Witkowski even forgot why he had come.

Suddenly we heard sounds in the distance, which gradually got closer to us. We saw German prisoners of war, torn, tired, dirty, with swastikas on the back and the front of their tunics, lugging huge sacks on their backs. Young armed Poles accompanied them and hurried them forward. They turned to tell us that the sacks contained tinned meat taken from a German storehouse, for the civilian population of the Old City. The Germans, bent double, were treading the same Zamenhof Street along which hundreds of thousands of Jews had been headed to the *Umschlagplatz* and thence to Treblinka. I looked at the Germans and thought to myself—the same street, the same helplessness, but one difference: the road to Treblinka is not for them.

Jan Witkowski stood and cursed. There was no foul expression he did not hurl at the Germans. He was even prepared to strike them. He had, in fact, raised a spike of metal he had found, all set to hit them over the head, and would have done so if the Polish guards had not stopped him. How easy it was to understand the anger of this simple man, whose nation and country had been utterly ruined. I just stood there helpless, feeling paralysed and overcome, looking at the angry man, the German prisoners and the silent ruins so filled with meaning for me.

Witkowski turned to me and said, "What do you think of that decrepit idiot?" pointing to an old, barefoot, bedraggled German. I jumped, for the words he had used for decrepit idiot were Hebrew. Was this for my benefit? I quickly remembered that many Yiddish and Hebrew words were now among the common derogatory vocabulary of some Poles, and they did not really know what the words meant. So I said nothing, just smiled.

The German columns passed and again we were alone in the street. I glanced over at Mila Street, at Muranowska Street, at Nalewski Street—all a heap of rubble. Mila Street was the worst; we could not even walk through it. Among the ruins stood the burnt-out shell of the last Judenrat headquarters, 21, Zamenhof Street. It was easy to walk in through the broken gateway. The building, which before the war had been a military prison, was divided by a series of courtyards. We walked through each of them. In the third courtyard, there were visible relics of the Jewish Uprising. On one side lay a heap of bones and ashes. What had happened here was easy to see. Mr. Witkowski, anxious to aid my comprehension of the scene, explained to me that the bones and ashes were those of Jews who had tried to revolt against the Germans. On the other side lay a heap of rotted clothing and mildewed shoes. Witkowski was afraid that the Poles, now busy fighting, might yet end up the same way.

Later, in the winter of 1946, I acted as an interpreter for the Anglo-American Committee of Enquiry into the problems of European Jewry and Palestine, when they visited the Warsaw Ghetto. I showed them this courtyard with its bones and ashes. They all removed their hats and paid silent tribute to the fallen heroes.

Witkowski and I spent long hours walking through the ruined streets. So far, my companion had found nothing that he considered of value. From time to time he saw a gaping hole which led into the cellars, and was anxious to go down and search, but I held him back as he might have been trapped among the debris.

In Dzielna Street we found an intact staircase which led into a cellar. Witkowski tore down quickly and disappeared, while I stood alone in the abandoned battlefield. In a few minutes he came up holding a postcard-sized photograph. He said to me,

"Have a look at this. That damn Jew looks just like our Jesus!" I looked and saw that it was a photograph of the well-known Rabbi, Judah Zlotnik. He was known as a scholar and linguist under the pen names of El-Zet and Avida. I had known him since childhood, as he was a native of my own home town. Also in the cellar was a collection of books which had belonged to the Ascola High School in Warsaw. Of course these things were valueless to Witkowski and I dared not exhibit the least interest in either the books or the picture. We left everything behind, but in 1945 I hurried back, found the things all intact, and took them away.

Witkowski was cross with me. We had wasted a whole day and found nothing useful. However, he was luckier later on. It turned out that the German meat warehouses were in the *Umschlagplatz* buildings and Witkowski took a few tins. He returned home triumphantly with the spoils of the day's foraging.

This was the only time I was able to visit the ghetto during the Polish Uprising. Within a few days, it was again occupied by the Germans, and from this base they fired steadily on all the houses in the Old City. The iron barricade erected by the foreign Jews proved a very good defence.

44. The Sewers

THE POLISH UPRISING in the Old City collapsed after one month. The Germans reoccupied street after street and the Polish fighters took to their heels into the main city sewers. Some groups went via the main sewer entrance to Zoliborz and some to the centre of town. The civilian population were ordered by the Germans to evacuate the Old City and were taken to a transit camp to Pruszkow near Warsaw. Fighting continued, however, in other sections of the city. In the Old City, the most vulgar and despicable elements of the population were again vociferous in their hatred of Jews, as if the failure of the Uprising could be blamed on them, almost non-existent though they were.

In the first days of the revolt, the Polish press had published a message from La Guardia, the Mayor of New York, to the Polish population. He appealed to the Poles to stand firm, assuring them that the free world was behind them. The Poles were proud and happy to read the news; they saw from it that, in spirit at any rate, they were not alone, that the world supported them in their fight against Nazism. But now, in these last few days, one could suddenly see leaflets pasted on doorways bearing just two words— "La Guardia—Jew". The old Nazi game was starting again.

It was a sad fate for everybody to leave the Old City, but saddest of all for the Jews who had managed to survive thus far. In the press of crowds running away, it was easy to spot the Jews, who stood bewildered, with nowhere to run. Friends were constantly stopping me in the streets, asking me what to do, what was the best way out.

While I was in the cellar at 13, Franciscan Street I heard a groan; someone was sitting on the steps outside. I sensed that it was a Jew. I saw a very old man with a yellow waxen face, utterly broken-down and wild-eyed. He moaned incessantly. People passed by, stared, and moved on. Who had the time or inclination to deal with the forlorn now? Even Jews who passed in the crowd avoided looking at him. They were fully occupied with their own problems and could do nothing to help him. Meanwhile the Polish fighters were withdrawing from the street. They assembled in our courtyard, hurriedly erected a barricade and decided to carry out one more resistance operation against the oncoming Germans. I watched this performance, and wondered how to extricate myself from the battle, lost before it was started.

Opposite the house, in the courtyard, stood the caretaker. During the whole of the previous month's heroic action he had indulged in hard drinking bouts and singing patriotic songs. He sidled up to me, smiled sarcastically and said, "The Jews will get their deserts from the Germans pretty soon." I knew whom he meant but there was no time to argue; I had my life to save. A controversy was raging in our cellar; should we surrender to the Germans, or carry on the fight? My friend, Ignacy Pulawski, sided with the group who wanted to surrender, feeling that there was very little alternative. Pulawski, tired and resigned after the month's battle, was downcast and tried to persuade us that the Uprising had been pointless, and that it would be even more pointless to waste more lives. I was disappointed and astonished to hear his argument. No Jew could have agreed with him, but one had to remain silent.

We were a group of twelve under his leadership and everyone, myself excepted, went out and surrendered to the Germans. I had little time left in which to make my own decision. One thing was clear—I would never voluntarily surrender to the enemy; that would be suicide. The longer one could hold out, the greater the hope of survival. Perhaps a miracle would happen. And it did.

I decided to leave Franciscan Street, and through underground tunnels and ruined cellars made my way to Swietojerska Street. I knew that my old friend, the lawyer Jan Piechowicz, lived there. I felt closer to him, at that time, than to almost anyone. I hoped and believed that he would not surrender and would perhaps find a way of saving both of us. I found him, and stayed with him at number thirteen for two days. All the houses around were blazing or smouldering; corpses lay in the streets and courtyards. Burials were not even thought of. Jan Piechowicz was as calm as ever. He stayed at home, ignoring the bombing and the fires; taking off his spectacles, he cleaned them very slowly and asked me, "Are you really worried? If you are frightened we must do something. But calmly, not on the spur of the moment."

In the meantime the Polish fighters were deserting this area too, and we two seemed to be left alone in the German-occupied street. To add to my misgivings, Piechowicz went out at night and promised to return in the morning. For me, sleep was out of the question. Suppose he rejoined the fighters and did not reappear? But at six o'clock on the second morning my friend bounded in to tell me we were saved; we were leaving the Old City at once. He held an official-looking document which had been given him by the Polish authorities, authorising him and ten members of the Editorial Board of the paper *Warszawianka* to escape through the sewers, which were normally used only by military personnel. My name was among the ten.

The entrance to the main sewer in Krasinski Square was already in German hands. We had to get to a side channel, and from there make our way into the main sewer. We hurried to the corner of Dluga and Kilinski Streets and there we found the manhole leading into the side channel. I was the happiest man in the group. This was the only way out for any Jew in the Old City and I had the luck to be able to take it.

Everything went well. We each held a lighted candle and slipped down the narrow metal rungs into the damp darkness of the narrow pipe. Piechowicz led the group and I brought up the rear. This channel, out of the mainstream and not used for years by the sanitary authorities, was cramped, dirty and muddy. We had to crawl on all fours. Our goal was the large main pipe which led from the Old City to Warecka Street in the centre.

We crawled laboriously, holding our candles. We had to rid ourselves of our possessions and most of our clothes, since the perspiration was pouring freely off us in the humid, airless tunnel. I suddenly had a strange, instinctive feeling that something was wrong, that we were crawling in the wrong direction. Piechowicz, the leader, did not realise that the route he was taking, swinging to the right, led directly into the Vistula. That meant the end—death by drowning. I shouted out to my predecessor and the message was passed on to the front. There was an argument and my fear increased. The Germans were in the street above us and, knowing that people had taken to the sewers, were throwing grenades down the manholes. Eventually everybody agreed to change direction. Their fate was now in my hands; I was appointed leader. We crawled for an hour which seemed like a year. Suddenly, we heard the sound of rushing water. No one knew what this meant—but there was no retreat. We went forward. Unexpectedly, the channel ended and I fell into a strong swirling current. I had landed on my feet, the water up to my waist. I saw a group of Polish soldiers and knew we had arrived safely. They were on the march from the Old City into the centre of town. Thank God I had decided to change the route, or we should all have died. Now we marched on with the soldiers. To be honest, this channel was paradise compared with the pipe we had just crawled through.

The water was waist-high, but at least we could stand upright. The current, however, was very strong, and we needed great strength to stay on our feet against the tide.

During the last hour of the march we were met by medical orderlies and nurses, who were expecting us. They showed us the way out into the town and treated the injuries of those who were lacerated. It was around noon. Our group of ten gathered together at the exit in Warecka Street and decided to enlist as a military unit with the proper authorities. Covered in mud, tired and hungry, we reached Moniuszko Street where there was an enlistment centre. As usual, Jan Piechowicz acted as our spokesman. We were all given hot soup and bread for lunch and I stayed close to him, feeling safer that way. While we were eating, I noticed that Kaminski, my friend from the Old City, was there. I was astonished. He was walking backwards and forwards across the room but, when he saw me, he backed away; very odd behaviour, I thought.

We waited impatiently for an officer to whom we could report, as we were anxious to be assigned to a fighting unit. We lined up in order of height and, as I happened to be the tallest, I was the first to give my name, and the place I had just come from, to the slim, elegant officer who eventually appeared. Everyone gave the same information and we awaited his reactions. He said with unbending stiffness, "All, except number one, are assigned to the unit in this area." He told me to leave at once. I could not believe my own ears. Piechowicz would intervene for me, I was sure, but he remained silent; why, I shall never really know. I wanted to ask the officer why he would not accept my services but I was afraid that questioning might make my position even worse. Again, as so often in the past, silence was safest.

I went into Marszalkowska Street and stood there, helpless. Now I understood Kaminski's behaviour. He, too, was frightened, and as a Jew did not want to be seen too close to another one.

I was later told by a sister of Ignacy Pulawski that he and his friends who surrendered to the Germans were shot by them.

45. The Uprising Collapses

IT WAS NOW OBVIOUS that further resistance to the overwhelming strength of the Germans could not last very long. No one realised this more clearly than the defeated people of the Old City and those few Jews who had escaped. Bitter argument raged among the fighters themselves, the left-wing group saying that the Uprising had started too soon and blaming the government in exile in London for giving the order, and the right-wing group castigating the Soviet army. A Soviet detachment was already encamped in the suburbs of Warsaw, on the far bank of the Vistula; they did nothing to help the Poles to gain their freedom, though they knew full well what was happening. Either way, Warsaw was dying, and would soon be under the yoke of the cruellest of dictators again.

It was early September, 1944. In the centre of the town the mood was still fairly optimistic; the population had not yet suffered the sort of attack which had completely ruined the Old City. But this would undoubtedly come. It was a matter of time. As for me, I stood helpless and forlorn in Marszalkowska Street rejected alike by God and man; or so it seemed to me after my experience in the enlistment centre. I stood waiting, but for what, I just did not know. The passers-by looked at me sympathetically. The mud of the sewers had dried on my clothes in hard cakes. It was easy to see that I was a victim from the Old City.

I remembered that in the first year of the war, before the ghetto had been walled off, I had often visited the Vilna Bank in Marszalkowska Street, where the director, Teivan, was a friend of mine. He had helped me a great deal in those early days and I had got to know all the bank employees, including the porter. I knew that Teivan had a house outside Warsaw, but the porter lived on the bank premises. This was the only friend I could think of at that moment. As soon as I got to the bank, I saw him. He took one look at me, shouted, "Get out at once!" and slammed the door in my face. My disillusionment after this second rejection may be imagined. I firmly believed that life for a surviving Jew was much worse at the centre of town than it had been in the Old City; and I stood in the street again with no prospects and diminishing hope.

I now bitterly regretted the loss of my two friends, Pulawski and Piechowicz, whom I had lost within the space of hours. Suddenly, something happened. In Boduen Street I met an elderly lady who noticed my sorry state and asked me sympathetically about the fight in the Old City, and what was going to happen to me. She was moved by what I told her and invited me into her house. This seemed like divine intervention at the eleventh hour. In her neat basement flat, I met other families who had escaped from the same quarter.

The welcome she extended to us all was a typical example of Polish hospitality at its best, and I felt reborn. I washed in hot water, a rare luxury in those days, put on the clean clothes she gave me, had a meal, and, most fortunate of all, was allowed to stay overnight. However, a brief conversation with the other people there was enough to convince me that, in general, the dislike of Jews here was, if anything, greater than it had been in the Old City. They had not the slightest suspicion where I myself was concerned.

This was the only night I spent in Boduen Street. Early the following morning a massive German attack was launched against this part of the town. Bombs fell in our vicinity and the house was totally destroyed. Again, I had to look for some form of shelter.

I knew that the Piotrkowicz family had a flat at 49, Marszal-kowska Street; I also knew that they were then at Skolimow with their parents. When I went to the house I found that the flat was occupied by a number of refugees from other parts of the town, but I decided to stay there nevertheless, introducing myself as one of Piotrkowicz's relatives. I was there for four weeks, until the Uprising finally collapsed. Again, many Jews took part in the fighting, but they did not communicate with each other as no one admitted his origin. People often talked about the responsibility borne by Jews and communists for the lack of Soviet aid during the Uprising.

As a member of the Civil Defence I did guard duty at night with one other man. We stood at the corner of Zbawiciela Square, gunfire raining down on us. Bombs, grenades and anti-tank guns exploded constantly, and in that inferno we were convinced that the end was near. An officer approached us; he had come from the front line, where the Polish soldiers were desperately battling with the Germans, not too far from where we stood. He cursed the Germans fluently but his most vehement oaths were reserved for the Jews. He told us that he had a few Jews in his unit who pretended to be Poles. They really thought they were deceiving everyone. He, however, could recognise them with ease—by their large, fat hands! I had become an expert on what were supposedly typical Jewish characteristics, having been informed of them by a variety of neighbours. Among other signs were the sorrowful eyes, the hooked nose, the large bat ears and similar fanciful attributes. Now I learned of a new feature—large, fat hands. My one comfort was that I could be happy about my own; they were merely skin and bone as a result of malnutrition. The last few weeks passed without any trouble.

There was one enemy, apart from the German attacks, that could have ended our lives. That was starvation, which was rife in the centre of town. The hunger which the refugees suffered was insupportable, particularly those who had neither acquaintance nor friend with whom to lodge; things were so bad that women could be seen at street corners holding up articles of jewellery and coins which they would gladly have exchanged for a scrap of bread. No one took any notice of them. Bread was scarcer and more valuable than gold. A neighbour who lived in the same house noticed that I could not drag myself upstairs to my room on the first floor, though he did not know that I had dysentery and had lost a lot of blood. Weak with hunger, I remained sitting at the ground floor entrance. Seeing me there, he offered help, and gave me a bag of dried rusks which he had kept for years in case of grave food shortage. He himself had enough to eat and he advised me to soak the rusks and boil them into a sort of porridge.

That, he said, would sustain me. I was overcome with joy, and I crawled slowly up and tried to boil the rusks. They were so old and dry that even boiling water did not soften them. I decided to pound them to flour with a mortar and pestle, but as soon as I crumbled them I saw, to my horror, large meal worms crawling out. I separated the worms from the meal, boiled the meal and ate the porridge. It saved my life.

Ten days before the Uprising collapsed I met a high-ranking Polish officer called Sobolewski. He took to me at once and enlisted me on active service. My duty was to lead a group of soldiers with a supply of food and arms from Wspolna Street to the district of Czerniakow which was still in Polish hands. The route lay through the Germans lines. We arranged to travel at night. Life was easier now since I was provided with rations which I shared with the other people at the flat. Returning one morning from Czerniakow to the headquarters at Wspolna Street, we found a pile of ruins where the four-storey house had been. In our absence a bomb had reduced it to rubble and the death toll had been very high. I lost contact with Mr. Sobolewski and was sure that he had been among the dead at Wspolna Street. Later, I discovered that I was wrong.

During the eight weeks of the Uprising I had no idea what had happened to my wife. She should have been at Piastow near Warsaw, but I could not be sure. Whatever had happened, I was thankful that she was not with me during those terrible days; she would never have survived.

To sum up the results of the Polish Uprising from the Jewish point of view: not only did it fail to liberate us, but our suffering was intensified and our hopes were at a lower ebb than at any time during the war.

46. The Time of Surrender

THE POLES CAPITULATED in October 1944. The Germans presented harsh terms to the leaders of the Polish Army, including the surrender *in toto* of all military groups. The whole of the civilian population of Warsaw was to abandon the city within the next few days. The town was in an uproar. But the gunfire and bombing had stopped, and the streets were packed with people, jumping from one mound of debris to another. Everybody was preparing to leave. The actual evacuation was carried out by the Germans and each individual had to pass through the transit camp at Pruszkow.

The state of mind of the remaining Jews can be imagined. This situation was similar to the one in the Old City when that area had surrendered to the enemy. This was not simple escape, but an organised passage through a German camp. There were two possible solutions, both very risky. The first was to leave with the population and hope not to be spotted in the crush. This would be difficult, as we had heard that the transit camp had a group called "The Heaven Brigade", a gang of hard, vicious men whose sole duty was to spot Jews and hand them over to the Germans, thus expediting the Jewish passage to "Heaven". The alternative was to stay put in Warsaw, hide in the ruins and wait for the final liberation. This was also complicated in the extreme. No one knew how long he would have to wait; winter was approaching; food and water were hard to come by; and, above all, to find a safe hiding spot which the Germans and others would not discover required great expertise.

It was difficult to decide what to do, but a ready answer presented itself. In the crush of people I met an old professional colleague of mine, with whom I had worked for a number of years in the Michael Kreczmar High School before the war. We greeted each other warmly and I told him my problem. He immediately suggested that as a member of the armed forces I join him, also an officer, and surrender to the Germans. I found it should difficult to consider such a course, but I was temporarily persuaded that it was the best thing to do. I agreed to go with him.

The next day we both went to Sniadeckich Street, two among thousands of soldiers standing in orderly rows. We saw nearby a small group of high-ranking German officers waiting to receive us. A priest in a white surplice was conducting a short service for the soldiers, and when he had finished we all joined in singing the Polish national anthem. The German officers stood to attention and saluted the leaders of the Polish Army. I stood aghast when I saw them so close, and sensed their hypocrisy and duplicity. Having mercilessly bombarded and ruined the city, they now saluted its national anthem. Unhesitatingly, I said farewell to my colleague and ran back into the rapidly emptying city. I could not surrender to the Germans and preferred to take my chance on whatever happened to me.

I was alone again, waiting for a miracle. The chance of meeting a group of Jewish friends from pre-war days was surely non-existent. But I saw a knot of people in a corner having a hurried discussion and, edging closer, I just could not believe my eyes. Four Jews! They were David Guzik, the Director of the American Joint Distribution Committee; Karol Popower, chief accountant to the Jewish community in Warsaw; a certain well-known socialist; and a member of the Jewish Underground Fighting Unit (JOB). We were all overcome with excitement and happiness. David Guzik thought that I had disappeared as a result of the plot organised by the Germans, when Jews in hiding on the Aryan side had been told to come to the Hotel Polski. They were assured that they would be sold passports and sent safely abroad. In actual fact they were sent to Auschwitz. I myself had believed the tale and was among those at the hotel, but my wife smelled deception, and her instinct saved our lives. Popower had been certain that my wife and I were taken to Treblinka in January 1943. I described the scene in Sniadeckich Street to them. They all agreed that I had been sensible to slip away, and they felt that sitting tight in the ruins and waiting for the Soviet offensive would be the safest thing.

Karol Popower suggested that I should join them; they had already found a well-concealed bunker where we could all stay. I told them that I would rather leave Warsaw. Having passed as a Pole for so long, my luck would surely hold out a little longer. Popower looked at me pityingly, saying that my nose was too great a risk! I stood speechless, compared his appearance with mine and decided that he was the one who was running risks. Perhaps that was why he wanted me to join him in hiding? Fear bred suspicion in those days. The others did not agree with Popower. Since I was confident enough, I should leave Warsaw if I could, although they chose to stay behind. As I said goodbye, Guzik pressed a coin into my hand. I did not know what it was. Later on I saw that it was a gold twenty-dollar piece. I had become a millionaire!

Karol Popower walked with me to 49, Marszalkowska Street and on the way told me how he and his wife had managed to survive. He himself was a very mild, inactive sort of man and so I was interested to hear his story. His daughter had been a university student in Paris before the outbreak of war, and had been shot there by the Germans. Her husband, Grzegorz Korczynski, a Pole, came back to Poland via various illegal routes and was now an active underground worker. It was he who had helped them. They had lost contact with him during the Uprising and had now decided to stay and wait for whatever end was in store. He still felt I was taking a big risk and advised me to stay with them. Korczynski, incidentally, is now (1968) a member of the Polish government, one of General Moczar's group.

We made our farewells in the hope of meeting after the liberation. I packed a few belongings and prepared to leave town with the crowds going to the transit camp.

The four people hidden in the ruins of Warsaw, I learned later, survived the most terrible hardships and near-discovery by the Germans. They were liberated by the Russians in January 1945.

47. The Flight from Warsaw

AT THE BEGINNING of October, 1944, the cold bitter winds and bleak days were more wintry than autumnal. We too were bleak, dark and wintry in our lassitude. No one even thought about a future any more. The inhabitants were packing and leaving Warsaw, and could be seen making their way with their pitiful luggage to the main line Western Station. They all went on foot, dragging and limping all the three-mile long journey. The Germans had laid on a train which went backwards and forwards from the station to the transit camp at Pruszkow. Everybody was trying to get away at dawn, and I wondered what the hurry was. My neighbours in Marszalkowska Street were also among the earliest to leave; only a few people were left in number 49. I was among them. I had plans of my own. I thought it would be better and safer to leave town in the afternoon. In the dimness of dusk it might be easier to escape detection. Another thing occurred to me. To leave alone would be dangerous; it might draw the attention of the Germans to me. I had to find a group with whom to go; in fact, to be one of a family. I was lucky enough to find company. An old man, who was also alone, agreed that I should go with him. He and I would be related.

After my escape from the Old City through the sewers I had been left without any possessions whatsoever. But it was important to collect a few bits of junk to carry with me, so that I would look like the others, a settled citizen, who had packed up part of his home before leaving to live elsewhere, and was carrying whatever was necessary and portable. I ended up with a rucksack on my back stuffed with heaven knows what, a suitcase in one hand and a rug over the other arm.

We both set out, well loaded. We had to go through a narrow gate, where German officers and Gestapo in plain clothes counted the file of people as they passed through and gave each one a loaf of bread. The old man and I passed through safely—a good omen. On the main road we were among tens of thousands of families. It was lined on each side by German soldiers, guns loaded and pointing, to prevent us from escaping into the open spaces and fields round Warsaw. We were still "under arrest". People under the weight of luggage moved slowly and would not be hurried. Each kept to his own pace, worried, quiet and obeying orders. I tried once or twice to ask a German if I could leave the crowd on the main road, using the pretext that I had relatives nearby. I had to stay where I was. Nevertheless I was happier than all the people marching with me. This was very different from my former march with the Jews, hurried and bullied on the road to Treblinka.

After about two hours, we arrived at the station. It was overcrowded, with everyone waiting for the train to Pruszkow. We were, as before, surrounded by armed Germans who took good care that we did not leave the station. I sat down with my old "relative", and we put our luggage down around us. I had to think ahead. Perhaps there was still some way of escape?

I asked the old man to excuse me, left all my luggage except the rucksack and moved towards one of the German officers, requesting that he allow me to cross the line to the opposite platform as I wished to go to the lavatory. People around stared at me, openly admiring my courage in so frankly addressing a German. He merely said firmly, "Zurück, zurück—Back, back." I had expected that reply. But I was desperate not to be on that train, so I decided to try again. I took off my rucksack, placed it near his feet, and begged him again to let me cross the line, pointing to the rucksack as I spoke. He looked down at the overstuffed bag, softened, and said I could go. I left him guarding one valueless item. The old man knew I was trying to get away, but he stayed put; I never saw either of them again.

I jumped down and crossed the line to the other side which was an empty platform. Suddenly, a man in civilian clothes, carrying a revolver and with a dog at his side, appeared beside me. His first question to me in German was, "What are you doing here?" One look at him and the revolver and the dog and I was speechless with fear. I stammered out why I had crossed, and pointed to the German officer on the opposite platform. He nodded and confirmed that I was telling the truth. The fellow moved off, and I made my way down the platform, trying to get as far from the station as possible. I walked into a field which adjoined the platform and met two Polish boys, aged about ten and twelve. They told me that they had been working all day with a group of labourers; the others had returned home by van, but they had inadvertently been left behind and had to make their own way home on foot. They had to get to Piastow.

When I heard that I was overjoyed. My wife had been hiding there, and I hoped she had stayed put. Perhaps I would be able to walk with these lads. I joined up with them, holding some of their tools and acting the role of a workman. The three of us began our journey.

It got dark very quickly as we were approaching the village of Wlochy. A woman appeared out of the gloom and warned us not to go any further; German officers were guarding the road into the village and were arresting all civilians. The two lads laughed and said they knew a side road, and could avoid the Germans by using it. It began to rain and it was well beyond curfew. Getting to Piastow was out of the question. I assured the boys that I knew the priest in Wlochy and that we would be able to stay at his residence overnight and go on to Piastow in the morning. We were also very hungry and I said hopefully that we would be well fed at the holy man's house. The idea of food appealed to them, and they readily believed all I said.

We went on walking through the fields. In the thick blackness we saw a feeble glow of electric lamps, which meant that people with torches were coming towards us. In a matter of minutes we were surrounded by a German patrol. An order was shouted: "Stop! Hands up!" I held on to the spade and said that we were returning home from work. One of the Germans snapped, "Identity cards." I took out mine, in the name of Jan Zielinski, and showed it to him, taking care that he noticed the swastika on the front cover. This, happily, was a military police patrol, not Gestapo or SS, so the sight of the swastika was enough to satisfy them about my identity. They asked no more questions but said we

were to get home as fast as possible as it was long after curfew.

We entered the priest's house by the kitchen, and the sight and
smell of food overcame us. The children could hardly wait for the
feast. As soon as the priest saw us he told us to get out. The
Germans had forbidden him to shelter any civilians as Wlochy
was so near to Warsaw and the front line. I appealed to his conscience, his sense of pity and his brotherly love. To strengthen
my arguments, I quoted some relevant passages from both the Old
and New Testaments, and I could feel the priest listening with
amazement and interest. Perhaps I was a priest in hiding who had
escaped from Warsaw? His attitude mellowed considerably. Of
course he would like to help all refugees, but he was terrified of
the Germans. I said we could not go out as it was long after curfew; it was pouring with rain, and I promised that we would leave
at the crack of dawn as we had to get to Piastow, where we
lived.

He took a candle and lit our way up to the attic. Food was not
mentioned, and I had neither the impudence nor the courage to
ask. The attic was filled with people, probably other refugees from
Warsaw; there were bodies wherever we stepped, but we saw no
faces in the dark. I counted the minutes to daylight. The boys were
hungry and complaining, but I could not help them.

While I rested there, I had another disturbing thought. When I
left Warsaw, I had changed my old jacket for a warmer one and
had forgotten to remove my twenty-dollar gold piece from the
pocket. Now I was no longer a millionaire; I was a beggar.

As the first streak of daylight appeared, we three set off again.
Everybody was quiet and sleeping, and no one saw us slip out.
After a short brisk walk, we arrived in Piastow. I said goodbye
to the boys and gave them the few coins I had with me. In fear
and trembling I entered the Krzosek-Miaskiewicz house where,
before the Uprising, I had left my wife. When I asked my friends
where she was, they merely said that she had gone. I was sure that
the Germans had taken her away, but later I was told that she had
gone on to another village with some relations of the family. The
danger at Piastow, near the front line, was too great, hence the

move. Where she had gone, they did not tell me, and I could not enquire too closely. The most important thing was that Henrietta was safe in her new hiding place.

48. Twenty Days in Piastow

THE TWENTY DAYS I spent in Piastow after I had escaped from the Germans were extraordinary ones. Danger was a normal condition of life in those days, but the three weeks after the Polish Uprising were remarkable because of the interesting and frightening company I had to keep. The active Polish communists who had always been associated with the Miaskiewiczes were continuing their fight against the Germans—in the same house as a group of Germans returning from the Russian front on their way home! The Germans had commandeered flats and houses and were now temporarily resident.

During my stay in Warsaw I was constantly aware of my good fortune in having a place to which I could go if I managed to escape from that ruined city; and, indeed, when I arrived at the address in Piastow I was welcomed with open arms by the landlady and her family. I felt at home and relaxed. Of course, many of them remembered me. The Polish fighters treated me as someone special, even as a sort of hero; they liked the idea of my surviving that purgatory, serving in the army and, above all, refusing to surrender to the enemy.

The Krzosek-Miaskiewicz house in Piastow was a centre of illegal activities. Many underground workers had stayed there, including some who had fought in the Uprising and managed to escape. They were all communists. The secret work done here was outstanding. No one was called by his name. Everyone seemed to be very mobile and there was a constant and varied stream of people passing through the house. One often heard them talking about a "surprise blood bath". This meant that a silent attack would be launched against the enemy—against German military units, the Gestapo, and, very often, collaborators. The operations were usually carried out at night.

There was a secret printing press in the house for necessary documents, which were all heavily stamped with a swastika; these were invaluable to the fighters. There also seemed to be plenty of printed news items and communiqués from other parts of Poland and the front line. It was here that I learned for the first time about the National Liberation Committee which was now working actively in Lublin.

My personal papers were also somewhat "amended" there. It would have been fatal if I had been challenged and made to show my identity card, which had been issued to me as a resident of Warsaw. To any German, it would have looked as if I were a surviving fighter of the Uprising. The printers asked me what changes I wanted. Did I want to be a German general, a police officer, a railway inspector? They could print anything. My request was modest; merely an authorised date and place stamp that would show I had been resident in Piastow for several months. This easiest of tasks was accomplished in minutes.

Living in close proximity to the communist resisters were the other inhabitants of the house, the group of Germans. The Wehrmacht soldiers had already been there for weeks when I arrived, awaiting their orders. Most of them were getting on in years and were beginning to comprehend that the "Thousand Years of New Order" they had been promised was crumbling round them. It was easy to see their disillusionment from their speech, behaviour and general appearance. Of course, their mere presence was a great problem. Among them were a few very young soldiers, who were obviously worried about all the activity and bustle in the house. They could not help noticing the constant stream of visitors. We were afraid of these youngsters; for them, Hitler was still God and Führer. They asked continually what all these people were doing. "Why don't they go out to work? Why don't they help in the fight against Jews and Bolsheviks?"

One of them was very aggressive; his eyes radiated viciousness. He once asked a young communist directly why he was so lazy and did nothing. The reply in Polish was so vulgar as to be unprintable. The German asked what it meant, and, we, in broken German, assured him that the Pole had said that everyone in the house was anxious for a German victory. He was satisfied with this reply.

For a number of days we closely observed two soldiers of a Hungarian unit attached to the German army. They were elderly and behaved differently from their comrades. We suspected, somehow, that they were Jews. The communists wanted me to ask them, but I refused, as it was too dangerous. One day when the two Hungarians were alone in the kitchen, deep in thought, one of the young Poles walked in and said, "Jews?" I was in an adjoining room, but I could hear everything. At first they pretended not to understand. But they eventually admitted that they were, in fact, Hungarian Jews who had enlisted as Aryans in order to save their lives. They went on to say that they were very concerned about their relations at home, and asked what had happened to Hungarian Jewry. They did not know that most of them had been murdered. After a few days the two Hungarians, with the rest of their unit, left Piastow. It was rumoured that they had been sent on for security reasons, as we were near the Russian front.

The few Jews hidden in Piastow at that time were suffering badly. The Pruszkow transit camp was nearby and the members of the "Heaven Brigade" were very active over a wide area, ferreting out Jews and handing them over to the Gestapo. Not a day passed without its fresh supply of victims. I remember well the day that five Jewish patients were taken out of Piastow hospital, four women and one man, and shot by the Germans. This happened after information received from the "Heaven Brigade". My neighbours were furious and determined to wipe out the informers, but no one could actually point them out.

In spite of the kindness and hospitality I encountered I was still afraid; afraid that I might be spotted by a collaborator, or by one of the Germans that were left. The nights were, perhaps, the worst of all. There could have been a sudden visit by the Gestapo to search the house. All the rooms and beds were occupied and I racked my brains to find some way of not staying in the house at night. Apart from the fact that it was very risky, there was simply nowhere to lie down.

There was an outside lavatory in the courtyard with a small attic above it. During the day a ladder was propped against the wall, for climbing into the attic; at night, it would be easy, once inside, to drag the ladder in. This was a first-class hiding place and I spent the twenty nights there. It was the safest sleeping place I knew. Every night when it was pitch black, I disappeared inside with my ladder and was the first person out in the morning. The only thing that worried me was that the Germans, frequent visitors to the lavatory, might suspect that I reclined above them. They never did.

I kept on asking if it would be possible for me to go and seek out my wife, but my hosts did not agree to my request. They felt that it might be dangerous, not only for me but for her and the people who were sheltering her.

The situation worsened from day to day. The young Germans often showed that they were suspicious of us and were open in their hatred of us. It was obvious that trouble was brewing. The Gestapo would be sure to call at the house, and then we would all be finished. The Polish fighters melted away one by one; no one knew or asked where they had gone. When the Gestapo eventually came one night, they found young Waclaw Miaskiewicz, the son, and no one else. He was arrested, but after pleading for him his mother secured his release from prison. I had already left the house at that time.

49. The Burning City

IT WAS THE END OF OCTOBER, 1944, and winter was fast approaching with its cold, wet, windy days. The weather made us feel even more dispirited. I was still at Piastow counting the days and waiting for some change in the circumstances, with only my faith and hope to sustain me. Penniless and having no contact with my wife, I relied simply on the kindness and charity of my hosts, but I could not suppress my frequent pangs of conscience about my enforced idleness at the expense of others, and the fact that I was putting them in danger. I sat around miserably, knowing I could not repay them.

I could not help remembering the gold twenty-dollar piece I had left behind in Warsaw and was constantly wondering how I could go back to retrieve my fortune. It was possibly still there in my jacket pocket. Suddenly an opportunity presented itself. The house in Piastow was often visited by nuns from St. Mary's convent in Hoza Street, friends of my host's daughter, also a nun. They had been forced to evacuate from Warsaw along with all the civilian population and had left large quantities of foodstuffs behind in their convent. They discussed this pretty often and, with their Mother Superior as spokesman, were trying to get permission from the Germans to go back to Warsaw to retrieve the hoard.

I wondered if it would be possible for me to join the nuns, if and when they went, and get my little fortune back. Under normal circumstances travelling with them would have been unthinkable, and even now to risk one's life for twenty dollars seemed mad enough. But it was, in fact, an essential undertaking, as I could not exist much longer without a penny to my name. Warsaw had been burning for weeks; the Germans were systematically burning street after street, and the red glow in the sky was visible from Piastow. If we *could* get back, I would surely be the only Jew who had returned to the capital after an adventurous and miraculous escape!

I often chatted with the nuns and suggested diplomatically that I was prepared to escort them and help them in their task. My hostess aided my pleas since I had confided to her my reasons for wanting to go, and had promised her ten dollars for my board and lodging. So it was all arranged and the nuns hired two horses and a cart which I was to drive. We needed another man to help load the goods when we arrived there, since speed was essential and we had to return the same day. We found him soon enough; a man called Tadeusz Wysokinski who, as a Warsaw citizen, had some business there.

We set out at 6 a.m.; two nuns, Wysokinski (who alone knew I was a Jew) and I. My appearance was now that of a professional coachman. I wore old tattered clothes and long riding boots, and tied a rope round my waist. I walked beside the cart carrying a long whip, holding the reins while the others rode. In this way we passed through the German guard post into Warsaw. I could hardly recognise the city. Not a soul in sight. Whole streets of houses in flames. Hundreds of Russian collaborators from the Vlasov army were on horseback everywhere and Russian was the prevailing language. If I had not seen Germans throwing incendiary bombs into the houses, I could have imagined that Warsaw was already occupied by the Russians. I thought of Nero burning the city of Rome to get inspiration and material for a poem; the Germans were burning Warsaw for no reason at all.

We were to go to St. Mary's Convent in Hoza Street, but I asked if we could stop first at 49, Marszalkowska Street. The nuns agreed and I turned the cart around. As we approached I could see that number 49 was in flames and the whole frontage had already collapsed; the others noticed it too, and wanted me to turn back, but I begged them to wait for a few moments. They stayed in the cart and I ran into the courtyard. The staircase was still intact, I noticed; and in seconds I was up in my old room where, in the wardrobe, I found my old jacket with the twenty-dollar piece in the pocket. Delighted with my find, I rushed out and we all went on to the convent. On the way there we witnessed a sad scene: two civilians being shot by the Germans in Marszalkowska Street. We pretended not to notice.

The work at the convent was hard and tiring and the sacks and boxes of food seemed as heavy as lead. It turned out that enormous quantities had been secreted in wall cavities; flour, sugar, spirits, tea and coffee, and various other commodities. We, of course, could hardly believe our eyes. Tadeusz Wysokinski kept on saying, "What a hoard, what a hoard." It took us hours to remove and load the parcels. The nuns had left us and gone into town, but we found it safer to stay in the convent precincts. Suddenly we became aware of a strange young woman in the courtyard, who wanted to talk to us. She said that she had stayed in Warsaw because of her brother, who was now lying injured in a cellar. She begged us to save both of them and take them out of Warsaw. It was easy to see that she was Jewish from her approach, her appearance, and the terror in her eyes. My companion, too, recognised this and agreed that we had to rescue them; also, that the nuns must be made to agree. We promised that we would do all we could, but had to tell her that everything depended on the nuns. They were the ones with a safe conduct, not we.

At first the two holy sisters did not want to take along two strangers; it was too risky, they thought, as the official pass gave freedom of travel to four persons only. They were finally persuaded, though they never dreamt that they were rescuing Jews. After we had dealt with all the foodstuffs, we got the sick young man out of the cellar and laid him in the cart. The nuns sat among the packages with his sister and my companion Wysokinski and I walked alongside. The boy groaned constantly to impress us with the severity of his injuries, but my friend and I realised that he was physically as fit as a fiddle—his only real sickness was being a Jew.

The nearer we got to the German guard post, the more frightened we became. Would we get out as easily as we had got in? We thought it would look better if everyone got off and helped push the heavily laden cart rather than let the tired horses drag the load. No sooner said than done. The young man sprang off like an arrow and everybody started pushing. The guard post was now manned by Russians on horseback. They were not interested in the pass we presented, and anyhow could not read the German words; they were more concerned with the contents of the sacks and boxes and searched for firearms. As soon as they found the bottles of spirit they went wild. Each of them took a bottle and speedily forgot about us.

In the darkness of early evening, we arrived back at Piastow, the nuns with their fortune, I with mine, and above all, with our two rescued souls, whose joy cannot be described. The young man and woman changed perceptibly. They spoke freely and could not thank us enough, the nuns, the coachman and his friend who had saved them.

The Warsaw ghetto in ruins, with a solitary
Christian church left standing
(*photograph by Robert Capa*)

"There is no longer a Jewish quarter in
Warsaw!"—SS General Stroop

Es gibt keinen
jüdischen Wohnbezirk
in Warschau mehr!

SS General Jürgen Stroop (in foregound), who conducted the liquidation of
the Warsaw ghetto

50. The Hero of Wulka Dankowska

EVENTUALLY, my hosts had to leave Piastow, and they agreed to take me with them to meet my wife. They stipulated two conditions: when we arrived at our destination, I was to behave like a stranger to her. This would be safer for all of us. All I had to do was to bring her greetings from an apocryphal husband who had disappeared at the time of the Polish Uprising. Apart from that, I was asked if I could get a horse and cart for the journey as they could not afford to pay for transport. This was easy for me since my rescue of the twenty-dollar piece.

I now learned for the first time where we were going; it was a hamlet of some twenty-five houses called Wulka Dankowska. There was three small towns in the vicinity, Grujec, Mogielnice and Blendov. The distance from Piastow was about a hundred kilometres. Going by train was too risky; the Germans would often stop trains en route and take all the men out for forced labour. So it was decided that we would take our horse and cart via the side roads and tracks, as main roads were filled with Germans. Tadeusz Wysokinski and another friend, Stanislaw Bukowski, as well as the driver of the cart, were to come with us.

The path we took led us through fields and forests, quicksand and acres of mud. The horse could hardly manage to drag through, and we often had to get out and raise the sunken wheels and push the cart onto safe ground. We were on the move for two days and arrived at the hamlet at night, when the whole area was dark and silent. It had been raining for some hours and we were soaked to the skin. We stopped at the first hut near the forest and were received with great hospitality by the owner, Jan Kowalski, and his wife and two daughters. They were related to the Miaskiewicz family.

Shortly afterwards, other relations appeared; my wife was

with them. Now I had to act the stranger. She was presented to me as Mrs. Antonina Jozwiack. I immediately told her that I had been with her husband in Warsaw during the Uprising, conveyed his regards, but regretted that I did not know what had happened to him. We both played our parts well. Not one of the strangers guessed that there was any relationship between us. We sat down to supper, Mr. Kowalski providing the vodka, and the atmosphere was festive; but I was waiting for an opportunity to speak privately to my wife. After the meal Mr. Kowalski took us into his barn where the new arrivals were to sleep. It was here that I had a chance to see Henrietta alone.

She told me about conditions in the hamlet generally. Everyone had tried to convince her that I was dead, as no one could have escaped alive from Warsaw. She ought to forget about me as fast as she could, for her own sake. I had to endeavour to lend support to this idea and maintain, as I had been instructed, that I had not seen her husband since the Uprising. . . .

Life seemed fairly secure in the hamlet, she said. It was a long way off the main road, there were few Germans around and, above all, the inhabitants were simple, ordinary, decent folk living a static rural existence. However, unexpected problems had arisen in the last week or so. After the Uprising a Polish officer had arrived in the village and had become over-friendly with all the peasants. He went from house to house asking endless questions and spent his evenings playing tunes on a comb, which delighted the young people. He had even been appointed deputy mayor of the village. My wife added that the officer had cast some odd glances in her direction and she had been terrified for the last few days.

As can be imagined, I did not sleep all night after this news. I would have to be circumspect with this deputy mayor, for he could be the death of both of us. I tried to quieten my wife, telling all that had happened to me and adding that great numbers of homeless families from Warsaw were wandering aimlessly around the countryside. In that kind of turmoil, the odd stranger would escape detection. We could only hope that we might remain here in safety till the end of the war. We both knew one thing—the hamlet was our last refuge. After this there was just nowhere to go.

Next morning, at dawn, we were awake and dressed. Now I could see that the hut was the first habitation in the village, right in the shadow of the forest. This was a consoling discovery. It was safer, being some distance from the other dwellings and the other people. But distance is hardly the word to use, since there was only one main street and a total of twenty-five huts. Everyone was bound to see us sooner or later.

After breakfast our first visitor arrived; a neighbour who was curious to see the new arrivals from the big city. She did not stop chattering and questioning us about Warsaw and about ourselves, and asking if Mrs. Antonina Jozwiak's husband were dead or alive. We answered all her questions but she seemed too much of an inquisitive busybody. We learned later that the chatterbox had two daughters, and was trying to catch a husband for one of them. As soon as we had got rid of her, two new guests arrived, with an official greeting for the Warsaw arrivals. They were introduced as the mayor, Antoni Ostrowski, and his deputy, the Polish officer. My initial reaction was sheer terror. My wife was equally frightened, wondering whether I would survive their scrutiny and questioning.

My terror was short-lived, however. As soon as the deputy mayor saw me he greeted me by the name Jan Zielinski, and called out, "Let me embrace you! How did you manage to escape from Warsaw?" Everyone was stunned and stared at us. The mayor stood open-mouthed and silent. It turned out that this Polish officer was Sobolewski with whom, during the last days of the Warsaw Uprising, I had served in the Army. Now I was suddenly a hero. Mr. Sobolewski told the assembled company of our exploits together and about the patriotic part I had played. The village and the mayor were all proud of me and glad to have me as their guest.

There could be no celebration without vodka, so we all sat down and drank one after another. Everyone soon mellowed. Sobolewski thought I should be found the best quarters possible, and a job. Then our first visitor turned up again from nowhere and assured the mayor that I should stay at her house—it would be a good home for me! I shuddered. I knew she might be regarding me as a prospective son-in-law. The mayor saved my life. He insisted that I stay with him. It would be an honour for him and for his wife to have me in their house. I discovered, too, that Sobolewski also lodged there, and so we would be under the same roof.

That same day I transferred myself to the mayor's house, got a job as a farm labourer and from then on drove into town with the mayor twice a week. His house had one room and a kitchen. He lived with his wife and child in the kitchen, while Mr. Sobolewski and I had two beds in the other room. We lived like this for many weeks, working together and spending the nights talking politics and playing cards, and counting the days to liberation. I worked hard but felt happy, feeling that freedom was not too far away.

At the beginning of January, 1945, the surrounding country-side lay under a blanket of thick snow. It looked like a Siberian landscape. Rumours started up in the village about my wife and me; there was some suspicion that we were Jews. Sobolewski, a very decent man, felt uncomfortable. He, after all, had praised me initially. He began to get frightened. Early one morning he packed a small case with his belongings, told the mayor he had to visit sick relatives for a brief while, and departed. He never re-appeared. It was obvious that he was afraid of staying under the same roof with me. The risk was too great.

51. Celebrations

LIFE IN THE VILLAGE was placid and nothing happened to disturb the monotony. Everyone waited for Sunday to arrive, for then they all went to church in the nearby town and, as soon as the service ended, made their way to the nearest pub where the week's gossip was analysed between rounds of alcohol. This visit provided topics for conversation for the rest of the week, ranging from politics to weddings. It was of special importance in winter, when the fields were covered with snow and there was little for the peasants to do.

However, some particular weekdays were different from the others, but they occurred infrequently during the year, and were celebrated with great festivity when they did appear. There was the day when one of the peasants killed a pig. The owner of the pig would invite all his neighbours for a drink in the evening and he would provide a meal made from part of the recently slaughtered animal. Early one morning in December, 1944, I heard that the village was preparing for a festive day. The animal himself proclaimed the event, for his shrieks could be heard all over the village as he was led struggling to the slaughter and even while he was being finished off. I cannot forget the scene when these two creatures, the pig and his master, met. Each tried to outdo the other, the pig in running away and the master in chasing after it. Witnessing such a brutal and tragic scene, I thought of all the cruelty which existed in the world—on a wider scale.

An hour after the killing, the owner of the pig went from hut to hut inviting his neighbours to celebrate with him. Among the first to be invited was the mayor of the village and he was reminded to bring his guest. That was I. I was very worried and wondered all day how I could get out of it. I knew that the food provided was fried pig's liver and blood sausage and nothing would have induced me to taste either of these foods.

At six o'clock in the evening we were all in our neighbour's house, helping him to make merry. A small paraffin lamp lit the only room and the proud housewife stood in the corner preparing the food. We sat around the table in a tight huddle, all the neighbours and their wives, while the host put bottles of home-produced alcohol in front of us, speedily followed by the steaming plates of offal. I started wriggling at the sight of it all. But how could I escape? My neighbour was Tadeusz Wysokinski, the only person there who knew I was a Jew. Thanks to him, I managed not to eat a morsel, since in the dim light I surreptitiously transferred the food to his plate, and took only bread and vodka.

It did not take long for the whole party to get drunk. Conversation flowed easily and the noise was deafening as bottle followed bottle. I tried hard to be one of the crowd, but could not forget for one second the gulf that separated me from them. There in that damp, dark room, among the drunken peasants and their wives, my imagination led me into another world. I saw all my relatives, my old friends, my teachers and colleagues, my students —people from that now vanished Jewish world. Nevertheless, I was not afraid of the villagers. We got on well together, passed leisure hours in each other's company and even went to church together. They treated me as one of themselves.

Only one member of that small community troubled me. He was a carpenter, a townsman who had moved into the country and considered himself to be much smarter than his rural neighbours. It was harder to deceive a townsman than a countryman, especially in the realm of the Jew acting the Catholic. This had contributed to the tragedy of the Jews in the big cities—they had been so easily recognised by their neighbours. The carpenter, Nowak, was much discussed in the village. People said that before the war he had been in prison for murdering his wife. At the outbreak of war in September 1939 he and other prisoners had been released. These criminal types were now freely living in a society which had forced the intellectuals and humanitarians to hide. Nowak, as a neighbour, was also sitting at the table, one of the guests at the celebration.

In the middle of the festivities, Nowak pushed aside his neighbours, stood up, banged on the table for silence and shouted out, "Quiet! Quiet!" The crowd, drunk and relaxed, went on talking at the tops of their voices. Nowak's voice rose again and could be heard above the din, "For me, all human beings are equal. Everyone has the right to live. But I admire truth." I shivered hot and cold all over. If our Mr. Nowak admired truth, there was danger in the air. Who knew with whom he had a score to settle! The host quietened his guests and Nowak started talking again. "The most important thing in life is truth. I hate to see people deceiving each other and living by lies. People say that he," pointing at me, "is a Jew! What is more, they also say that Mrs. Antonina Jozwiak is not only Jewish as well, but his wife!" (Fortunately she was not among the guests at the party.) Nowak continued, "I mean no harm in saying all this. We don't mind if a Jew stays alive, but we must know the truth."

The crowd, flustered, listened and said nothing. I watched my neighbours closely to see how they would react. Suddenly Ostrowski the mayor jumped up, grabbed a knife and screamed out angrily, "Let me get at him! I'll kill him on the spot!" I turned to look at the mayor. Whom did he want to kill? Me? He continued, "What! You throw such insults at my best friend? You call that patriot a Jew?" I was stunned, yet smiled as if nothing had happened. I realised that my fate could be decided right away. Other neighbours tore the knife from the mayor's hand and the din started again among the drunken crowd. The host banged on the table, quietened his guests and said, "Why don't we ask Jan Zielinski himself what he has to say?" The crowd agreed. I had not bargained for this, but I had to think fast. I stood up and said quietly. "To be quite honest, Mr. Nowak has behaved very badly. By talking like that he could endanger everyone in the village. But as you can all see, he is dead drunk and cannot be held responsible for what he says. When he sobers up he is bound to regret it." It cost me great effort to utter these few words and I sat down wearily. Now I had to wait and see how they would take it.

The guests seemed to subside quietly but the celebration had obviously been disturbed. Shortly afterwards the peasants and their wives dispersed to their own homes. But the basic situation remained unchanged since an important question had remained unanswered. Everything hung in the balance.

I left the house with the mayor and my neighbour Tadeusz Wysokinski. (Tadeusz was an electrical engineer. Although Henrietta and I had not known him very long, he had always shown us considerable sympathy and compassion.) Outside, a snow blizzard was raging. We clung together and just managed to stay on our feet, not even knowing if we were taking the right path as everything was under a thick carpet of snow. The mayor was still furious at Nowak and persisted in talking about him. "What scum! He should be taught a lesson! I know the only way—he should be shot!" It was all too simple for the mayor. He had a pistol at home and the body could be weighted down with a stone and thrown into the local river. It was obvious to me that this plan of action would be a fatal mistake. Nowak was a married man and had a number of children who would speedily inform the police. I said to the mayor: "We can't do that sort of thing—all the men in the village would be in danger. For one Nowak the Germans would shoot or deport all of us."

We came to an agreement. At midnight the mayor went to Nowak's house and dragged him out of bed. He informed him on behalf of the village that he held him personally responsible for anything that might happen in the future to any of the men in the district. Should the Germans come to inquire about Jan Zielinski or Mrs. Antonina Jozwiak, he would know that Nowak had informed them, and the penalty for that was death. Nowak stood shivering in his underpants and listened without a word. The mayor, of course, was fully convinced that not only was I not a Jew, but that I knew nothing about Jews. Nevertheless the village buzzed with gossip about us two suspicious characters.

It was our good luck that all this happened just a few short weeks before the liberation. It seemed that Mr. Nowak also got a fright. He thought it more prudent to remain silent and save his skin.

52. Three Towns

FATE HAD DECIDED that Sobolewski and I should stay as guests of the mayor of Wulka Dankowska for nearly three months. Although the mayor was generous and hospitable and never asked us to help him in his work, we nevertheless felt that we could not go on accepting his many kindnesses without offering something in return. There was plenty to do. In autumn the farmyard was to be cleaned and the cattle-stalls and the pig-pens washed down.

There was firewood to be chopped and there were general tasks connected with the day-to-day running of a farm; so we did anything and everything to please the mayor and his wife.

The peasants' attitude to Jews was interesting. Jews had been close neighbours of these villagers for hundreds of years and had engaged in trade and barter with them. They were friendly and helpful to each other, but a great gulf existed between the Polish peasants and their Jewish neighbours in the surrounding small towns. Those three months in the village opened my eyes; I learned what the peasants really thought. It was not a question of straightforward hatred or traditional antisemitism; Nazi propaganda of the usual bizarre type hardly ever reached these far-flung isolated hamlets. It was rather a question of total estrangement. To them the Jews seemed beneath contempt, an odd, strange group from another planet. This attitude was most clearly revealed when I lived as one of them and moved freely among them.

Not far from the village there were three small Jewish towns, Blendov, Mogielnice and Grujec. For many years the inhabitants had lived and worked intimately with the village folk. When the Jews in the towns had been wiped out some two years previously, news of the destruction quickly reached the village. Even now it was still discussed, but as if the Jews had been gone for centuries. The general reaction was indifference and it was hard to imagine that any amicable co-operation had ever existed. The villagers did not know in detail what had happened to the Jews, but they wondered if they would ever come back, since many of them owed the Jews money. This last troubled them greatly.

Practically every Friday the mayor and I went to Mogielnice for market-day. We mingled freely with the people and visited many homes; we saw everything, chatted to everyone. The signs of former Jewish habitation were visible everywhere. The old Jewish shops were there, the burnt-out synagogue, the desecrated cemetery; and in the houses, Jewish household goods were being freely used. The market square was always packed. The stall-holders were new, and the German police walked among them maintaining law and order. In the pubs, one often heard the Jews discussed, but always in contemptuous terms. I shuddered as I listened.

I had never been to Mogielnice before. But on all my Friday visits I was aware of a sadness, a quietness that hung over the deserted alleys. The market square teemed with activity, but the side streets were empty and brooding. One felt that something was missing.

Blendov was no different. I went there mainly during the week, not on market-day, and then the hushed somnolence was even more noticeable among the burnt-out ruins of former Jewish homes and prayer-houses. Often the streets were completely deserted, but for me they were peopled with ghosts. But as far as I was concerned there was another problem connected with Blendov. Our village belonged to the Blendov parish and every Sunday the village would go to Mass there. It was hard to get out of going with them. The church stood in the town centre, near the market-place. It was a favourite meeting spot. Everybody knew everybody else and a stranger was soon subjected to close scrutiny, in the church and outside. When people in the village were suspicious of me, they eyed me even more closely in church, to see if I could follow the Mass as to the manner born. I was aware of this, and tried hard to act as naturally and effectively as possible. I succeeded. Tadeusz, my good and trusted friend, told me that the peasants were pleased with me; I just could not be a Jew!

The third town, Grujec, was the same. Sorrowful silence prevailed here, too. It was farther from our village, so we did not visit it so often; but I remember one visit especially, when I saw some Germans leading a Jewish woman and two children into a field. Children and adults ran behind screaming and shouting. Two months later I stood at the graveside of this unfortunate woman and her children.

I often thought about the three towns while I worked in the village. Would it not have been possible to have saved some of the Jewish population and hidden them in the surrounding villages? Could not some have been hidden in the forest? It was noticeable that the Germans, who visited the populated areas from time to time, hardly ever went into the forest. In fact, two Soviet officers,

escaped prisoners of war, had been hidden in the nearby wood for
some time. They came out into the village occasionally, as they
relied on the peasants for sustenance. Although the peasants were
Catholics and far from being communists, they willingly helped
the two Russians, always giving them milk and bread and other
foods as they were available. This attitude was a natural facet of
their generous natures. Informing the Germans about the Russians
was unheard-of and unthought-of. I often met these Russians and
talked with them. They always felt calm and certain of survival,
and they did in fact, live through their ordeal.

Each time I spoke to these charming and intelligent men, I
could not help asking myself one question. Would any Jew in
the three little towns have risked hiding in the forest? Would
he have been able to feel secure about the attitude of his neighbours? The simple, friendly peasants would surely have been
ready to save some of their unfortunate neighbours if they had
been told about the open hospitality of the former Polish kings
towards the Jews; if they had been taught the liberal attitude of
some historians and statesmen towards the Jews in the past; if they
had known what some famous Polish writers had said about Jews.
All this was unknown to them. Simple and illiterate people, they
were vulnerable to indoctrination and they knew that the Jews
were filled with sin and immoral. That is why they treated the
Jewish catastrophe as a casual fact.

53. Village Life

IN THE LAST FEW WEEKS before liberation the Russian front line
was very near the village—in fact, the Russians were encamped
outside the town of Warka, on the opposite bank of the Vistula,
about 30 kilometres away. We waited daily, with bated breath,
for the liberating forces to reach us, but every Jew stayed well
hidden and was still terrified. Though we were so near to freedom,
each day was rich in "incidents", some of them tragi-comic.

On one frosty Sunday morning the mayor and his family, invited to lunch by his mother-in-law, left for a neighbouring village. I, virtually as a member of the family, accompanied them. The mother-in-law, a devout Catholic, always remonstrated with Ostrowski for his apparent lack of devotion. He had greeted her with a simple good morning, and not with the words, "Let us praise His name". She was very pleased with me, since I had made the correct remark. I would never have dared forget!

During lunch, our hostess kept saying that the village people should be willing to learn from those from the big city, for they were both kind and religious. She cited me as an example of the best sort of townsman, and also mentioned the lodgers she had staying with her. They were good Catholics too. They were an elderly woman and a child, both from Warsaw. It was a pleasure for her, she said, they were so kind and God-fearing. Her son-in-law should model himself on them. They were even now in their own room and had not joined the lunch party as they were still deep in prayer. I was most interested in her story of the very religious lodgers. Were they perhaps fellow-sufferers, as frightened as I was? After lunch, the mayor very gently opened the door leading into their room. We saw an elderly woman and child kneeling before a table with a picture of the Mother and Child. There was also a crucifix and other pictures of saints. One glance at the two drooping figures convinced me that they were Jewish.

A few days later I saw the old woman and the child walking in the fields between the two villages. I always pretended not to notice them, but it was easy to see that both were in a state of constant terror. It was not until much later that I knew that the old woman was frightened of the guest brought by the mayor to his mother-in-law—the officer from Warsaw who would be sure to recognise them as Jews. That was I of course; she had seen me many times in the village. The truth emerged a year later. The same woman came to my office in Warsaw and asked that the child, a Jewish orphan, be sent abroad with other children. I was then General Secretary for the Council of Jewish Communities in Poland, and in that capacity managed to send about five hundred homeless children abroad.

There was always a problem in the village over the consignment of food which the farmers had to hand over to the Germans. At certain times, a stated amount of grain, livestock and dairy produce had to be delivered. From time to time, Germans from the nearby town appeared, to check that the goods were assembled. Of course, nothing ran smoothly as some of the farmers sabotaged the trucks of food. They were not concerned with German orders and preferred to sell the food on the black market. Officially, the mayor of the village was its spokesman and he was the one to have direct dealings with the Germans. Naturally the Germans came to his house and spent hours going over the accounts. For me, this was purgatory—I often had to accompany the mayor and the Germans out on their tours of the neighbouring farms. They were afraid of being attacked by partisans hiding in the woods, particularly in the winter darkness, and would keep on asking if Jews or partisans were hidden nearby. Then from time to time suspicious-looking characters would appear in the village dressed in German uniform—they were Russian officers sent over to investigate matters.

One very cold day in January 1945, during a heavy snowstorm, when the outside world was deserted, I was working busily out in the stables. Suddenly an elegant two-wheel carriage appeared, drawn by a pair of white horses. Two young German officers jumped down and started questioning me. I pretended not to understand German. They were asking about German patrols in the area and how the local population treated the Germans. Luckily Benjie, the five-year-old son of the mayor, was with me. He was a precocious lad and well up in local affairs. Seeing the Germans, he wanted to run away, but they quietened him by giving him chocolate, and asked if they could lodge overnight at the mayor's house. I was not enthusiastic and advised them to go over to the miller's house, as it was larger and much more comfortable. They took my advice and went. That same night they met up with a German patrol, and so we found out that they were two Russians from the Warka camp.

Otherwise, life in the village could be very monotonous. Our stay there started with teeming rain and the countryside was turned into a sea of mud. Frost and snow blizzards followed. Conditions were Arctic. The days were short and the nights long and dark. There was, of course, no electricity. For me it was pleasurable to go out and walk in the forest, in its unspoiled peace and beauty.

My fellow lodger, Mr. Sobolewski, was full of new ideas. He decided that lots of reforms were needed in the village; he wanted the peasants to remember in later years that people from the big city had at one time lived among them. I begged him to save his schemes for happier days. But he would not listen; he was very stubborn and insisted on pushing ahead. For instance, there was no such thing as a lavatory in the village. No one even knew of the existence of such amenities. There was not even a privy midden. Each person used his own initiative and his own back yard. Sobolewski was anxious to build a lavatory for the mayor and his family, but Ostrowski and his neighbours regarded this idea as some sort of outlandish madness, saying that since their forefathers had managed so well without for centuries, so could they. I helped Sobolewski and we built a wooden structure, with a door. Inside was an earth closet with a proper seat. When it was finished, it was a nine-days'-wonder in the village. All the neighbours came to look and they smiled. One bright fellow said it could only be a Jewish discovery. My heart sank.

Occasionally, I had to walk to Blendov. The road was through the forest and I was glad to go on an occasional errand for the mayor. So as not to be conspicuous, I wore blue denim trousers, an old jacket and wooden shoes. Once, in December 1944, I was walking through the forest when a heavy snowfall set in, and in seconds I could no longer see the path. Snow clings to wood and hardens quickly. I tried to tear the lumps of snow off my wooden shoes, but could not. I was slipping about and could not stay upright. The snow got thicker and harder on the soles and I seemed to grow taller and taller on these unnatural platforms. There was not a soul in sight and I was terror-stricken, thinking my end was near. Suddenly the two Russian prisoners-of-war, who had been hiding in the forest, appeared on the scene. I knew them quite well. They, of course, knew all about snow adhering to wood and told me it was dangerous to walk in wooden shoes now. Laughing, they said the only thing to do was to go straight into town and have leather soles put onto my wooden ones. That was easier said than done: I took one tentative step and fell flat on my face. The Russians, in spite of the risk, helped me to the edge of the forest and on to the road. I got a lift in a passing cart to Blendov and in a few hours was back in the village in my newly-soled shoes. Later the Russians had a laugh at my expense in the village. They said that without them I would have reached Heaven, both because my shoes were getting higher and higher and because I would soon have died of exposure.

Christmas was a great worry to me. For the first time in my life I had to celebrate this festival as an intimate member of the mayor's family. I was particularly frightened of the Christmas Eve dinner, at which many traditional customs were observed; I had heard of them, but had never taken part. Luckily I managed to imitate the other members of the family so effectively that the dinner passed without incident. Afterwards some neighbours appeared, bringing with them their lodger, Mrs. Antonina Jozwiak. A large cart was harnessed with four farm horses and we all piled in. A young colt, unbridled, ran alongside. Whipping up the horses, we all raced through the village, singing carols at the tops of our voices. I was afraid a German patrol would catch us, since it was well past curfew. Happily we survived the noisy freezing ride. I cannot forget the white silent countryside, the glittering frost and the sound of the horses' hooves. We covered many miles at great speed, the little colt running free all the way. This was the mayor's Christmas hospitality to the guests.

At long last came that prayed-for moment of liberation which ended our five years of hell.

54. Liberation

THE DAYS STARTED WITH GUNFIRE—to us the stirring music of freedom. The window panes rattled with its vibrations every morning. It was now January, 1945. I lay alone, frozen stiff in my room after Sobolewski had departed so suddenly. It was six o'clock in the morning, and dark outside; the atmosphere was restless with sounds of conflict. Everyone was woken up by the daily morning symphony, which went on for an hour or two before silence reigned again. This pattern of events continued until 16th January, when the noise lasted for almost half a day; everyone knew that something momentous was about to happen. The long awaited liberation was drawing closer and closer.

Life proceeded as before in the village of Wulka Dankowska. The inhabitants had their own way of explaining the morning sounds, but no one knew with any certainty when the liberation would take place. No accurate news reached the village about outside events.

I decided to go to Blendov. Arriving there in the afternoon, I found it quiet and peaceful, as on any grey winter's day. The German police were walking about the streets and German officers were sitting in the pubs drinking beer. Suddenly the silence was shattered by a barrage of gunfire that grew steadily louder. This was a certain sign that things were moving, but I was afraid of asking too many questions. I got back to the village at dusk and saw cartloads of Germans arriving in front of the mayor's house. They went inside, put their rifles down in the passage and asked for hot tea. They were tired and frozen; just one glance at them was enough to show us what turn events were taking. There was surely some unusual activity in the immediate vicinity. Our neighbours in the village were inquisitive and wanted to see these new guests. In seconds they were all seated together, the peasants and the Germans all drinking and smoking—and saying nothing.

The silence was meaningful, and was broken only by repeated gunfire.

Sitting there with them, I wanted desperately to do something— my final act in this war which was about to end. I thought it might be a good idea to steal the rifles which the Germans had left in the corridors and take them prisoner. We might lock them in the barn till we were freed. I told the mayor my bright idea, but events then moved so rapidly that we did not manage to carry it out. A German officer on horseback appeared and ordered his comrades to leave the house and the village instantly. They were gone in a matter of minutes.

Now the gunfire started up on all sides and flares lit up the sky above the village. We heard the whine of machine-gun bullets and we seemed to be in the middle of the front line. The usually phlegmatic peasants were somewhat disturbed now. The gunfire continued throughout the night, and everyone was wide awake and worried. The main road was three kilometres from the village and we heard tanks moving along at all night. Nobody knew if they were German tanks retreating to the west or Russian tanks chasing the Germans.

Next morning, at about seven, my friend Stanislaw Bukowski from Piastow appeared in the house. He suggested that we should both pluck up courage and go out onto the main road, to see whose tanks they were; I agreed. It was still grey and half dark and snowing heavily. We took the forest path and accidentally came upon two dead Russian soldiers, recognisable by their uniforms. When we got to the roadway we saw to our joy that the tanks were Soviet ones. They moved forward with a column of soldiers marching on each side, bayonets fixed. Bukowski, as a communist, was overcome with happiness and hope. He wanted to know how I could be so indifferent and just stand there and look—it was impossible to tell him. I could hardly believe that the end of the war had really come—but had come too late for the Jews. And how could one start life again now?

Standing there, Bukowski pointed to one of the marching Russian soldiers and said, "Look, that one is probably a Jew. You go over and greet him and ask him what happened here last night." No sooner said than done. I rushed up to him and said, "Are you a Jew?" He replied with the foulest of Russian curses— not only was he a Gentile, but he was openly antisemitic. He even raised his bayonet to strike me and I, terrified, ran back to my friend. He, poor fellow, stood there open-mouthed and seething with fury; he had not expected me to get that sort of reception.

That was the first welcome we received on that historic day of January 17th, 1945. As we were not far from Blendov, we decided to go into the town to see what was happening there.

It was silent and shuttered, without a soul in the street. The local population were awaiting a different sort of liberation. They hoped that the Polish government in exile would set them free. The market square was filled with thousands of Russian soldiers, playing on mouth organs and performing Cossack dances. The ground was frozen hard and sparkled with frost, and it was not yet fully light. The Russians provided a gay scene with their expertise and agility.

We heard that a Russian commandant had taken over the local police station and that all the official buildings were already occupied by a new band of administrators. In spite of my earlier rebuff, I decided yet again to take the risk and make contact with the commandant. In a few minutes I was sitting in his office. He was a delightful young man from Rowne, and we conducted an animated conversation. I will never forget that talk; after years of murder and horror I felt relaxed and secure. He told me what had taken place in our neighbourhood in the last twenty-four hours. The Germans had been encircled unawares and with such speed that they had all been taken prisoner. Some had tried to resist and were shot. Their bodies were, in fact, lying in the streets. He knew all about the Jewish catastrophe, as he had been through many former Jewish towns and villages and had found them emptied of their inhabitants. When I told him about my difficult position, he asked what he could do to help me and my wife. I asked for only one thing—a pass to travel to Warsaw. Naturally I gave him my real name, Michael Zylberberg. He looked at me in surprise and said it would be better for me to use the false one for the time being. He gave me a travel pass in the name I had used for two years—Jan Zielinski.

At noon, we returned to the village. By this time everyone knew what had occurred during the night. I managed a quiet chat with my wife and told her about all that had happened with the commandant. We both decided to pose as Catholics for a little while longer, and continue to act like mere acquaintances. Leaving the village immediately was out of the question; winter was raging and our clothes were inadequate. I was still in my wooden shoes. In addition, there was no transport, and anyway we had nowhere and no one to go to. The thought of Warsaw terrified both of us.

That same evening, a number of Soviet cavalry divisions rode through the village. It was an unforgettable sight as they raced westwards towards Berlin. We stood for hours watching their brilliantly-coloured uniforms, their immaculate elegance, and the separate designs and insignia of each regiment. From time to time one of them would stop and ask, "Did any Jew manage to stay alive here?" It was obvious that they were Jews, and deeply concerned for the fate of any survivors. Sadly, I stood there in my silent distress among the peasants. I was still in hiding.

Two months later, I returned to Warsaw alone. I arrived there early in the morning. The whole town was in ruins, all the houses burnt to the ground. Apart from the soldiery, there was no one to be seen. All the civilians were living in Praga, on the other bank of the Vistula. This quarter had been liberated by the Russians for some months now.

I was in no hurry. It was obvious that none of our relatives would be among the liberated. I decided to postpone my walk into Praga and went instead on a personal pilgrimage into the ruins of the former ghetto. It was as silent as the grave. The whole area lay under thick snow. The whiteness, which should be a symbol of purity, frightened me. Under that whiteness flowed a sea of innocent Jewish blood. I wandered aimlessly over the ruins. There was no recognisable sign of what had once existed there. It was eerie and terrifying. Without realising it, I found myself at what used to be the cemetery at Gensia Street. Here I felt a sense of relief. It was all so familiar to me. In fact, I felt here as if I were amongst the living, not the dead. The names on the tombstones were names of people whom I had known in prewar years. They were Rabbis and writers, colleagues and friends. I stood at the single stone erected to the three famous writers Peretz, Dinensohn, Anski. I read the words—the poem of the Sabbatical and Festival Jews—which I, four years before, had recited in Janusz Korczak's orphanage.

All the people buried here, everyone who had been in the ghetto, seemed to come to life again. I felt almost sprightly here, much better than in the silent ruins. The cemetery wall had been destroyed—it seemed to break down the division between the two worlds of life and death.

I walked back through the ruins of the ghetto. My footprints were clear in the snow, and they were the only ones.

Bibliography

1. Ringelblum, Emanuel, *Notes from the Warsaw Ghetto*, New York, 1958.
2. Kaplan, Chaim A., *Scroll of Agony*, Translated from the Hebrew by Abraham I. Katsh, London, 1966.
3. Wdowinski, David, *And We Are Not Saved*, New York, 1963.
4. Goldstein, Bernard, *The Stars Bear Witness*, New York, 1949.
5. David Janina, *A Square of Sky, The recollections of a childhood*, London, 1964.
6. David, Janina, *A Touch of Earth, A wartime childhood*, London, 1966.
7. Goldkorn, Dorka, *Erinnerungen an den Aufstand in Warschauer Ghetto*, Berlin, 1960.
8. Seidman, Hillel, *Togbuch fun Varshever Ghetto*, Buenos Aires, 1947.
9. Turkow, Jonas, *Azoi iz es gewen*, Buenos Aires, 1949.
10. Mark, Bernard, *Walka i Zagłada Warszawskiego Ghetta*, Warszawa, 1959.
11. Mark, Bernard, *Der Aufstand im Warschauer Ghetto, Entstehung und Verlauf*, Berlin, 1957.
12. Berg, Mary, *Warsaw Ghetto, A Diary*, New York, 1945.
13. Mazor, Michel, *La Cité engloutie*, Paris, 1955.
14. Bernstein, J. and others, *Ghetto, Berichte aus dem Warschauer Ghetto, 1939–45*, Berlin, 1966.
15. Blumental, Nachman, and Kermish, Joseph, *Resistance and Revolt in the Warsaw Ghetto*, Jerusalem, 1965.
16. Wulf, Josef, *Die Liquidation von 500,000 Juden im Ghetto Warschau*, Berlin, 1961.
17. Goodman, Philip, *The Warsaw Ghetto Uprising, A Resource for Programming*, New York, 1963.
18. Litai, Chaim Lazar, *Muranowska 7, The Warsaw Ghetto Rising*, Tel Aviv, 1963.
19. Tushnet, Leonard, *To die with Honor: The uprising of the Jews in the Warsaw Ghetto*, New York, 1965.
20. Aurbach, Rachel, *Mered Getto Varsha*, Tel Aviv, 1963.
21. Stroop, Juergen, *The Report of Juergen Stroop concerning the Uprising*

214   *Bibliography*

    in the Ghetto of Warsaw and the liquidation of the Jewish residential area, Warsaw, 1958.

22. Kermisz, Josef, *Powstanie w Ghecie Warszawskim*, Lodz, 1946.
23. Lubetkin, Zivia, *Die letzten Tage des Warschauer Ghettos*, Berlin, 1949.
24. Rudnicki, Henryk, *Martyrologia i Zagłada Zydow Warszawskich*, Lodz, 1946.
25. Robinson, Jacob, and Friedman, Philip, Drs., *Guide to Jewish History under the Nazi Impact*, New York, 1960.
26. Freedman, Philip, *The Bibliography of the Warsaw Ghetto*, New York, 1953.
27. Neustadt, Melech, *Hurbn un Oifshtand fun di Yidn in Varshe*, Tel Aviv, 1948.
28. Iranek-Osmecki, Kazimierz, *Kto ratuje jedno zycie . . . Polacy i Zydzi, 1939–45*, London, 1968.
29. Borwicz, Michel, *L'insurrection du Ghetto de Varsovie*, Paris, 1966.
30. Yivo Institute for Jewish Research: *Life, Struggle and Uprising in the Warsaw Ghetto*, Exhibition, New York, 1963.
31. *Warsaw Ghetto Uprising: A reel of a Nazi Documentary film showing life in the Ghetto and scenes of the Uprising*, New York, Arista Film Services, 1963.
32. Czerniakow, Adam, *Warsaw Ghetto Diary*, Jerusalem, 1968.
33. Mortkowicz-Olczakowa, *Mister Doctor (The Life of Janusz Korczak)* London, 1965.
34. Sylvanus, Erwin, *Korczak und die Kinder*, St. Gallen, 1959.

Warsaw's Jewish Population: Statistics

Date		
1430	120	
1764	1,365	
1781	3,532	(In the same year, there were 5,000 Jews in Praga near Warsaw. This town had a total population of only 6,700 people)
1792	6,750	
1800	9,724	
1808	11,911	
1810	14,601	
1812	8,000	
1831	31,384	(25 per cent of the total population)
1837	36,413	
1840	37,039	
1845	43,820	(27 per cent of the total population)
1851	43,176	
1857	40,922	
1864	72,000	
1870	89,318	
1881	127,917	
1884	145,000	
1887	150,558	
1897	212,892	
1900	219,128	
1902	263,824	(36 per cent of the total population)
1910	306,061	(39 per cent of the total population)
1914	337,074	
1917	343,263	(41 per cent of the total population)
1921	322,000	
1931	352,659	

1934   354,000
1939   350,000   (33 per cent of the total population)
1940–1942   500,000   (including those sent in by the Germans
            approx.   from the provinces and abroad)
1943—before the Uprising—50,000 approx. (Between July 1942
            and April 1943, most of the Jewish
            population was exterminated).
1943—after the Uprising—officially, there were no Jews in War-
            saw. There were, however, a few
            thousand in hiding.

Sources

1. *Encyclopaedia of the Jewish Diaspora: A Memorial Library of Countries and Communities.* Warsaw. Ed: Itzhak Grünbaum, Jerusalem, 1953 (Hebrew)
2. *General Yiddish Encyclopaedia.* Vol. 4, New York, 1950
3. *The Jews in Poland.* Vol. 1, New York, 1946
4. *Historia i Literatura Żydowska.* Vols. 2 and 3, M. Balaban, Warsaw, 1925
5. *The History of the Jews of Warsaw.* Vols. 1, 2 and 3, J. Shatzky, New York, 1947, 1948, 1953 (Yiddish)
6. *Jewish Warsaw.* Ed: M. Rawitch, Montreal, 1966 (Yiddish)
7. *Megilath Poilin.* Leo Finkielstein, Buenos Aires, 1947 (Yiddish)

Index

Illustration on the last page is:

Detail from the Memorial to the Heroes of the Warsaw Ghetto, by the sculptor Natan Rappaport. It stands on the site of the former ghetto

Major Henryk Ivansky, known as "Bistry". This gallant officer of the Polish Army assisted the Jews before and during the ghetto uprising

General Bor-Komorowski, commander of the Warsaw Uprising, 1944